The Development of a Revolutionary Mentality

Library of Congress
Symposia on the American Revolution

The Development of a Revolutionary Mentality

Papers presented at the first symposium, May 5 and 6, 1972

Library of Congress   Washington   1972

Library of Congress Cataloging in Publication Data

Library of Congress Symposia on the American
     Revolution, 1st, 1972.
     The development of a revolutionary mentality.

     1. United States—History—Revolution—Congresses.
I. United States. Library of Congress. II. Title.
E204.L53   1972   973.3′11   72-11849
ISBN 0-8444-0045-9

Library of Congress Advisory Committee
American Revolution Bicentennial Program

John R. Alden
James B. Duke Professor of History, Duke University

Whitfield J. Bell, Jr.
Librarian of the American Philosophical Society

Julian P. Boyd
Editor of The Papers of Thomas Jefferson, *Princeton University*

Lyman H. Butterfield
Editor of The Adams Papers, *Massachusetts Historical Society*

Jack P. Greene
Professor of History, The Johns Hopkins University

Merrill Jensen
Vilas Research Professor of History, University of Wisconsin

Adrienne Koch
Professor of History, University of Maryland (Deceased)

Aubrey C. Land
Research Professor of History, University of Georgia

Edmund S. Morgan
Sterling Professor of History, Yale University

Richard B. Morris
Gouverneur Morris Professor of History, Columbia University

Preface

With Congressional support, the Library of Congress has undertaken a varied program, using as its theme Madison's phrase "Liberty and Learning," to mark the observance of the Nation's Bicentennial. Projects include the preparation of guides to contemporary source materials in the Library and bibliographies on the American Revolution, documentary and facsimile publications, exhibits, and other activities. Under the direction of the Assistant Librarian of Congress, the American Revolution Bicentennial Office in the Library has responsibility for carrying out or coordinating these programs.

It seemed to the Library that one of the most important contributions it could make to the observance of the Bicentennial would be to provide a vantage point from which present-day historians could view the implications of the American Revolution from the perspective of 200 years. Moreover, it seemed valuable for this and future generations to publish these views in a form that would allow their broad distribution and preservation.

With this in mind, the Library, with the advice of a committee of distinguished scholars, planned the Library of Congress Symposia on the American Revolution, a series of five annual conferences, each considering one aspect of the winning of American independence. The first of these symposia was held at the Library on May 5 and 6, 1972, based on the theme "The Development of a Revolutionary Mentality." This volume contains the papers presented at that time.

The symposia and this publication were made possible through a grant from The Morris and Gwendolyn Cafritz Foundation, established by the late Mr. Cafritz, Washington realtor and philanthropist. Through this grant the Cafritz Foundation, which fosters cultural, educational, and developmental activities in the District of Columbia, has made a significant and lasting contribution to the understanding of the American Revolution.

ELIZABETH E. HAMER
Assistant Librarian of Congress

Contents

The Development of a Revolutionary Mentality

Richard B. Morris began his teaching career in 1927 as an instructor in history at the City College of New York, where he taught for 22 years. He joined the Columbia University faculty in 1949, served as chairman of the history department, 1959–61, and since 1959 has been the Gouverneur Morris Professor of History.

Professor Morris holds a B.A. degree from the City College of New York, M.A. and Ph.D. degrees from Columbia University, and an L.H.D. degree from Hebrew Union College. He has been a visiting professor and lecturer at many universities in the United States and abroad, including Princeton University, the University of Hawaii, and the Free University of Berlin. In 1961 he received an appointment as a Fulbright research scholar at the University of Paris.

Among Professor Morris' many publications are Government and Labor in Early America *(1946),* The American Revolution, a Short History *(1955),* The Spirit of 'Seventy-Six *(with Henry S. Commager, 1958, 1967),* The Peacemakers; the Great Powers and American Independence *(1965), awarded the Bancroft Prize in history,* The American Revolution Reconsidered *(1967),* The Emerging Nations and the American Revolution *(1970), and* America, a History of the People *(with William Greenleaf and Robert H. Ferrell, 1971). Professor Morris is principal investigator of the papers of John Jay and is a member of the Library of Congress American Revolution Bicentennial Program advisory committee.*

Introduction

RICHARD B. MORRIS

I THINK I VOICE THE GRATIFICATION of all American historians that this first of a major series of symposia commemorating the Bicentennial of the American Revolution should be convened at the Library of Congress. How fitting indeed! We historians have enjoyed over the years the bountiful resources of this library, which owe so much to the vision of Thomas Jefferson and which have proved essential, nay indispensable, to almost every enterprise in the field of American civilization.

You may remember that when Washington assumed command of the army in Cambridge, he wrote his brother: "I am embarked on a wide ocean, boundless in its prospect and from whence perhaps no safe harbor is to be found." Some of us, perhaps, facing a series of five annual symposia analyzing all aspects of the great Revolution and culminating in 1976, may feel very much the same. What results we will reach and whether we will achieve a consensus is indeed a matter of speculation. But it is a great intellectual challenge, and I for one am willing to take the risks.

A few years ago I lectured at a number of universities in Yugoslavia on the American Revolution. My views must have seemed quite unconventional to someone reared in a Communist country, and one of the students asked me: "Professor Morris, do all historians in America agree with your interpretation of the American Revolution?" I replied: "You must remember that the United States is a democracy, not a totalitarian country, and, regrettably, quite a number of historians differ with me and are permitted to be quite vocal about it."

The fact is that on virtually every aspect of the American Revolution historians continue to exercise their privilege under the Bill of Rights to disagree. Some historians, most recently Jacques Ellul, do not even consider our War for Independence a revolution at all but a rebellion which rejected the immediate past but favored a former and more satisfactory past. Historians who take this position regard the American Revolution as having no future and no influence. I need not say that some of us would vigorously dissent from so parochial a view.

What is more, we are not even in accord upon when the Revolution began and when it ended. Some would agree with John Adams, who observed retrospectively that the American Revolution "was effected before the war commenced." Others would prefer Benjamin Rush's oft-quoted observation that "there is nothing more common than to confound the terms American Revolution with those of the late American War. The American War is over, but this is far from being the case with the American Revolution. On the contrary, but the first act of the great drama is closed."

If historians cannot agree when a Revolution started, when it ended, and if it is still continuing (as some hardy spirits insist), it is little wonder that there should be no unanimity on whether the Revolution was political or social, conservative or radical.

On one fact historians are agreed, however, and that is that independence was secured by the peacemakers in Paris in 1783. But even though we all grant that the Revolution was, first and foremost, a war for independence, there is no consensus about whether it serves as a model of a successful war of liberation against a colonial power. Critics of America's so-called neoimperialist stance would contend that in 1776 we were not a colonial people in the present-day usage of the term—that is, we were neither a nonwhite race nor an underdeveloped country. Others who see the American Revolution as offering the prime example to peoples emerging from colonialism are perhaps embarrassed that our present posture little accords with our historic professions.

And, so, just as the American Revolution divided Englishmen on both sides of the ocean, split Whigs and Tories, and fractured the united front of the patriot party, drawn as it was from so many diverse social, economic, and regional levels, the controversy about its shape, purpose, and consequence still arouses scholars to fever pitch.

One thing is clear. The American Revolution occurred in a period of extraordinary innovations in the realm of political ideas and institutions. Nor did these ideas emerge *in vacuo*. Some have traced them to Biblical and classical times. Others to the commonwealthmen of Cromwell's day, or to the Whig theorists of the Revolution of 1688, or to the emerging republican thought of English radicals in the generation before the American Revolution. If the ideas of the Enlightenment were contagious, then the Founding Fathers came down with heavy doses of the disease.

Henry Steele Commager received his Ph.D. degree in European history from the University of Chicago in 1928. He began his teaching career in 1926 at New York University, where he taught for 12 years. From 1938 to 1956 he served as a professor of history at Columbia University. In 1956 he joined the faculty of Amherst College as professor of American history, a post from which he retired in 1971. He has continued his association with Amherst as professor emeritus and Simpson Lecturer.

Professor Commager served as lecturer on American history at Cambridge University in 1942, Pitt Professor of American History at Cambridge in 1947, Harold Vyvyan Harmsworth Professor of American History at Oxford University in 1952, Gotesman Lecturer at Uppsala University in 1953, and special State Department lecturer to German universities in 1954. He has also held appointments as Richards Lecturer at the University of Virginia (1942), Zuskind Professor at Brandeis University (1954), Commonwealth Lecturer at the University of London (1964), and Harris Lecturer at Northwestern University (1964). In addition, Professor Commager has taught at universities in Israel, Italy, France, and South America and has received honorary degrees from many colleges and universities in the United States and abroad.

Among Professor Commager's many historical studies are The Growth of the American Republic *(with S. E. Morison, 1930 et seq.),* Documents of American History *(1934 et seq.),* Theodore Parker *(1936),* Majority Rule and Minority Rights *(1943),* America in Perspective *(1947),* The American Mind *(1950),* The Blue and the Gray *(1950),* Living Ideas in America *(1951),* Freedom, Loyalty, Dissent *(1954), for which he received a Hillman Foundation special award,* The Spirit of 'Seventy-Six *(with R. B. Morris, 1958),* The Nature and Study of History *(1965),* Freedom and Order *(1966),* Search for a Usable Past *(1967),* Was America a Mistake? *(1968),* The Commonwealth of Learning *(1968), and* The Discipline of History *(1972). He is coauthor, with Richard Morris, of the* Rise of the American Nation *series (30 volumes to date.)*

On the subject of the development of a revolutionary mentality our first speaker possesses unusual qualifications. Long a student of the history of ideas, of the rise and transformation of American nationality, and of constitutionalism, he is equally renowned for his devotion to civil rights, to minority rights, to the lucid exposition of Jeffersonian principles in Hamiltonian times, an enterprise that has at times required a good deal of courage. In short, no living scholar in America has given us a more forceful example of how to apply the ideas of the Founding Fathers to contemporary problems. It has been my good fortune to have collaborated with him over the past 20 years in editing a few dozen volumes in a historical series, but, for my own part, my most felicitous collaboration was in the preparation of a big documentary volume called *The Spirit of 'Seventy-Six*. Many people in this country regard Henry Commager as the living incarnation of that spirit today.

America and the Enlightenment

HENRY STEELE COMMAGER

My theme can be put simply and succinctly, though I am aware that simplicity is deceptive and succinctness suspect. It is this: that the Old World imagined the Enlightenment and the New World realized it. The Old World invented it, formulated it, and agitated it; America absorbed it, reflected it, and institutionalized it.

Intellectually 18th-century America was very much part of the European Enlightenment—particularly in its English, Scottish, and French manifestations; indeed, philosophically Europe and America may have been more nearly one world in that era than in any since. Almost everywhere the philosophes embraced a common body of ideas, subscribed to a common body of laws, shared a common faith. They were all natural philosophers —what we call scientists—and if they were not all trained in science, they were fascinated by it and dabbled in it: Voltaire, who early provided a simplified Newton; Goethe, who wrote learnedly (if mistakenly) on optics; Priestley, who invented not only Unitarianism but oxygen and soda water and wrote a history of electricity; Struensee, who was after all a medical doctor; Lord Monboddo, who anticipated organic evolution; and in America the members of the Philosophical Society—Franklin, Jefferson, Rittenhouse, Dr. Rush—and elsewhere a Manasseh Cutler, who combined botanizing with empire building, a Hugh Williamson, who was both doctor and ethnologist as well as historian, a Benjamin Thompson of Woburn, Mass., who became Count Rumford of the Holy Roman Empire and founded the Royal Institution in London and endowed the Rumford Chair of Natural Sciences at Harvard College.

They accepted the Newtonian world governed by laws of Nature and (if you wished to make gestures, as did Jefferson and Voltaire, or more than gestures, as did Newton himself) of Nature's God. They accepted, too, the principle of the sovereignty of Reason, and the axiom that Reason could penetrate to and master the laws of Nature and of God, and that it could persuade men to conform to them, not only in philosophy and ethics, but in politics, economy, law, education, even in art and literature, for they knew that:

> All are but parts of one stupendous Whole
> Whose body Nature is, and God the soul.

And they accepted—even those who like Albrecht von Haller had no use for its author—Voltaire's dictum that "God has given us a principle of universal Reason as He has given feathers to birds and fur to bears." It was Reason that guided the legal thinking of Blackstone and of his greatest critic, Bentham; Reason that reorganized the national economy in Austria and Prussia along cameralist lines; Reason that provided the arguments for the Declaration of Independence; and the great Jacques–Louis David announced that "the genius of the arts needs no other guide than the torch of Reason." Looking back over half a century, Jefferson celebrated the animating principle of his age:

We believed that man was a rational animal. . . . We believed that men, habituated to thinking for themselves, and to follow their reason as guide, would be more easily and safely governed than with minds nourished in error and vitiated and debased by ignorance.

Faith in Nature and in Reason was one of the common denominators of the Enlightened Despots too (an absurd term, that, but we seem to be stuck with it), and of the philosophes they sometimes attracted or seduced to their courts: of Frederick in Prussia, Leopold in Tuscany, Joseph in Austria, Catherine in Russia, Gustavus III in Sweden, or Charles in Baden;

of Pombal in Portugal, Campomanes in Spain, Struensee in Denmark, Tanucci in Naples, Goethe in Weimar, even, off and on, Turgot or Necker in France; and certainly of American philosophes like Franklin, Jefferson, John Adams, and Tom Paine.

From Newtonian premises there followed, logically, a passion for order that regulated almost every form of expression. "Order," their most representative poet had told them, "is Heav'n's First Law," and they made it theirs (at least when not too inconvenient), for they yearned to be in harmony with the will of Heaven. How they organize, how they codify, how they systematize and classify, and all Nature falls into order at their bidding! Thus Linnaeus imposed a *System of Nature* on all flora and fauna and Buffon on almost everything else in his prodigious *Histoire Naturelle*; thus the Encyclopédistes, not content with organizing knowledge in the greatest of literary enterprises, ultimately reorganized it all in the *Encyclopédie Méthodique* (eventually in 201 volumes). René Réaumur devoted six volumes to classification of insects; Albrecht von Haller gave five volumes to *Flora Helvitica* and eight to human anatomy: and the Baron d'Holbach organized everything into an ambitious *Système de la Nature*. Bentham tried to codify the laws of England; Americans for the first time systematized not only laws but rights in their constitutions; the Comte Real de Curban analyzed the science of government in eight volumes, and Filangieri created a science of legislation in six, and the Duc de Luynes devoted a lifetime to drawing up an orderly social register for the French aristocracy in 17 volumes. Order, too, presided over the chamber music of Mozart and Haydn, the gardens at Versailles and Schönbruun, the palaces and country houses of Eigtved in Copenhagen and Robert Adam in Edinburgh and Jacques Gabriel in Paris; order controlled the brush of Canaletto and the chisel in the hands of Thorwaldsen.

A third common denominator of the Enlightenment was both a prerequisite and a product of the first: commitment to freedom of the mind —freedom from religious and social superstitions, freedom from the tyranny of the church, the state, and the academy, freedom to follow the teachings of science and of reason wherever they led. From this followed inevitably war upon those institutions that threatened freedom; *écrasez l'infâme* was, symbolically at least, the rallying cry of the Old World Enlightenment, though not of the New, for the New had no *infâme* to crush. Jefferson's affirmation was even more appropriate than Voltaire's *cri de coeur*: "I have sworn upon the altar of God, eternal hostility against every form of tyranny over the mind of man." Outside America, few would dare take in quite that much territory.

They knew what to do with their free minds, too. Even more than the men of the Renaissance they were launched on voyages of discovery of new worlds, new ideas, new peoples, new societies, new civilizations, new laws; new flora and fauna, new and brighter stars in the skies and new and darker recesses of the human mind, new aspects of nature and of human nature, all their most representative figures participated in this great enterprise. They sailed with Captain Cook and Joseph Banks (that great entrepreneur of ideas who was to head the Royal Society for 42 years) to chart the transit of Venus and find new continents, or they walked with the Connecticut Yankee John Ledyard from Paris to Yakutsk to ascertain the common ties that bound Asia and Alaska; they gazed at the heavens with Herschel, who doubled the known universe, or experimented with Priestley and Lavoisier in their chemical laboratories; with Winckelmann and Niebuhr they uncovered ancient civilization and with Colden and Bartram and Jefferson himself they studied the American Indian. With Montesquieu and Gibbon they explored the causes of the rise and decline of empires and with Christian Wolff and Voltaire and William Chambers they penetrated to the mind and the art of China; with Rousseau and Pestalozzi they opened up a new world of childhood, and with the fantastic Lord Monboddo they promoted the orangutan to his rightful place in the chain of being.

The philosophes shared a fourth passion and commitment: a humanitarianism which imagined and fought for the abolition of torture and the amelioration of the barbarous penal code that still disgraced the statute books of even the most civilized nations; an end to the Inquisition; improvement in the lot of the peasants and the serfs; the abolition of the slave trade and even of slavery itself—all that might contribute to the enhancement of private and public happiness. It is here that the Enlightenment blended almost imperceptibly into Romanticism, for what more romantic notion than that society had an obligation to advance the happiness of its people.

Their ultimate objective was, of course, to liberate the minds and the energies of men to achieve what providence had so clearly intended: to conform so perfectly to the laws of Nature that the errors, evils, and corruptions which had for so long afflicted mankind would vanish and man would enter a new golden age. An exhilarating program this, but the agenda of the philosophes was not really exhilarating; it was almost wholly negative. For the philosophes were helpless against the weaponry of the state, the church, the Inquisition, the law, the military, even the universities, which bristled on every quarter of the horizon. These could not, in fact, be overthrown; they had to be circumvented, placated, or won over, and in most countries the energies of the philosophes were devoted to the elementary task of survival: Diderot cast into jail, and the *Encyclopédie* banned; Voltaire in hiding or in exile; Rousseau on the run; Tom Paine outlawed; Pietro Gianonne languishing in jail in Turin for the audacities of his *History of Naples*; even the great Buffon forced to retract all those portions of his *Histoire Naturelle* to which the church objected. Before the philosophes could begin the great task of reconstruction there had to be a clearing away of censorship, the Inquisition, torture, corruption, arbitrary power, of a hundred evils, each one, it seemed, hydra-headed.

And how was this to be achieved? Not through suffrage, for except in England and Holland and some of the Swiss cantons there was no suffrage to speak of, and not much even in these more liberal countries. Not by an appeal to public opinion, for even if here and there an elitist opinion existed, there was really no way in which it could be made politically effective. Not by working through the church or the universities, for these were an essential part of the establishment, and outside Scotland and Holland and a few of the German states the universities were moribund. No, the great enterprise of liberation and freedom, if it was to succeed, must be adopted by princes and monarchs who were themselves philosophes.

2

All the philosophers, European and American alike were trained on the classics, and all knew Plato's prediction that there would be "no end to the troubles of states, or indeed, of humanity itself until philosophers became kings in this world, or until those we now call kings and rulers, really and truly become philosophers." There were no philosophers who were kings, though Goethe may have imagined himself one, but all the kings were philosophers, or pretended to be, and if they were not they hastened to attach philosophers to their courts so they could be respectable. Consider Frederick of Prussia: Did not Voltaire and Diderot and La Grange and Maupertuis all testify that he was a philosopher, the very paragon of philosophers? Or consider the Empress Catherine, the Semiramis of the North, who combined the wisdom of Solon and the justice of Lycurgus (so said Diderot, who ought to know; so said the Baron Grimm, who gave her all the literary gossip for 22 years). She invited Voltaire to her court, in vain. She invited d'Alembert to tutor her grandson, and when he refused to come she imported Frédéric de La Harpe, the young man who had won a prize for the best address on *Peace*—just what most interested Catherine! She invited Beccaria from Milan to reform her penal code, but nothing happened; she even invited Diderot to draw up a model educational plan, which he did and which she promptly forgot. And up in frozen Stockholm was the brilliant young Gustavus III. He had seized the reins of power, he had knocked Hats and Caps off hard Swedish heads, he had established freedom of the press and ended torture, he founded the Swedish Academy, he patronized poets, he adored the opera, and the muses rewarded him with immortality by turning his murder at a masked ball into just such an opera as would have delighted him. There was Karl Friedrich of Baden who wrote a book on physiocracy and was so enlightened that he determined "to make his subjects into free, opulent and law-abiding citizens whether they liked it or not," and there was Karl August who ruled Weimar and made that tiny duchy a showplace of Europe, what with Goethe and Schiller and Wieland, to say nothing of Herder and Fichte.

And where the kings were not sufficiently enlightened their ministers were: the mighty Pombal, who rebuilt Portugal after the Lisbon earthquake, and the incomparable Sonnenfels in Vienna, the son of a rabbi—think how enlightened that was of Maria Theresa—and, for a time Campomanes in Spain, and Struensee in Denmark, who turned everything upside down in 14 months, and in Munich Count Rumford, who introduced not only order but potato soup into Bavaria. It was all a mutual admiration society, too. The kings indulged the philosophes, and the philosophes extolled the kings: all worked together for the happiness of man.

It is all too good to be true. Alas, it is not true. The play is so brilliant, the lines are so witty, the plot is so intricate, the setting so polished, the costumes so splendid, the music so enchanting, that we sit enthralled through it all. Then the last lines are spoken and the actors depart, and the lovely tunes are only an echo lingering on in our mind, and the whole thing is a dream. We look at the stage and it is no longer a stage: it is no longer the Seville of the Barber, but of the Inquisition; no longer the London of the *Beggar's Opera*, but of Gin Alley; no longer the Naples of *Così Fan Tutte*, but of Ferdinand IV crushing the revolution and the romantic Prince Caracciolo hanging from the yardarm of Lord Nelson's *Minerva*; no longer the Venice of Goldoni, but of Giorgine Pisani who had appealed to the populace against the inquisitors and was allowed to rot in jail. Catherine no longer plays the role of the Semiramis of the North, and

when the wretched Alexander Radischev wrote a book depicting the hard
lot of the serfs she shipped him off to Siberia; worse yet, she relegated all
her busts of Voltaire and Diderot to the basement! In Copenhagen Struensee was drawn and quartered for violating the queen, and the privileges
of the nobility; and over in Norway a leader of the peasants, Christian
Lofthuus, deluded himself that he had a mandate from the king to speak
for his countrymen: he was chained to a block of stone in the fortress of
Christiania and left to rot.

Now what everybody does—così fan tutte—is no longer to play at love
and war. No, the bugles that sound are real bugles and the drumbeats will
soon roll across the whole of Europe. The armies march and Poland is dis-
membered. Now Goldoni is dead and the Venetian Republic is no more,
and Wordsworth can write those elegiac lines. In faraway Quito the patriot Dr. Espejo is tortured to death for reprinting the Declaration of the
Rights of Man, and in Portuguese Bahia four radicals who called for equality in a democratic republic are hanged. Now the comedy is over and
reality takes charge. That is why it is not Giovanni descending into Hell
while all the happy swains and maids stand singing in the courtyard, or
Floristan rescued from the dungeon, or Casanova with still another con-
quest; in the end it is "infuriated man, seeking through blood and
slaughter his long lost liberty," seeking it but not finding it. In the end
the philosophers were not kings, nor even next to kings: Turgot dismissed,
Necker dismissed, Count Rumford expelled, the mighty Pombal disgraced,
Johann Moser languishing in solitary confinement, Struensee beheaded,
Brissot guillotined, Condorcet dead in that jail in Bourg-la-Reine, a copy
of Horace in his pocket. The few who retained power—Sonnenfels in Austria, Tanucci in Naples, Pitt in London, for example, conveniently forgot
most of their liberal principles for, like their masters, they were frightened
out of their wits by the spectacle of liberalism translated from philosophy
to politics.

All true enough, but not in America. The waves of reaction lapped at
that distant shore but did not inundate it. It was Jefferson who was elected
president in 1800, not Aaron Burr or Fisher Ames.

3

Americans had no kings, not after they had toppled George III anyway.
No kings, no aristocracy, no church in the Old World sense of the term,

no bishops, no inquisition, no army, no navy, no colonies, no peasantry, no proletariat. But they had philosophers in plenty. Every town had its Solon, its Cato, and certainly—as John Trumbull made clear in *M'Fingal*—its Honorius. And if the philosophers were not kings they were something better—they were the elected representatives of the sovereign people. In America, and in America alone, the people had deliberately chosen to be ruled by philosophers: Washington, Adams, Jefferson, Madison in the presidential chair; a Bowdoin, a Jay, a Jonathan Trumbull, a Franklin, a Clinton, a Pinckney, a Livingston in the gubernatorial—and you can go on and on. Now that we are busy celebrating the traditions of the Revolutionary era, this is one tradition we would do well to revive—philosophers as kings.

Not many of them, to be sure, could devote all their energies to statecraft or philosophy, for they were more like Cincinnatus than like Caesar, busy with farming or the law, and in any event they lacked the courts, the churches, the academies, the universities, which provided so much of the patronage, the nurture, and the security for philosophes in the Old World. Yet politics and "universal reformation" were not an avocation with them, a game, as one so often senses they were in the Old World. They were a serious matter, a lifelong consecration—just what Jefferson meant when he wrote, for the Congress, that "we mutually pledge to each other our lives, our fortunes and our sacred honor," just what Washington meant in his eloquent circular letter to the states of 1783:

The foundation of our empire was not laid in the gloomy age of ignorance and superstition, but at an epoch when the rights of mankind were better understood and more clearly defined, than at any former period, the researches of the human mind after social happiness have been carried to a greater extent, the treasures of knowledge... are laid open for our use, and their collected wisdom may be happily applied in the establishment of our forms of government.

In America, and perhaps alone in America, statesmen and philosophers were not required to curry favor with capricious monarchs or to bend the knee to power (I am not forgetting the counterargument of a capricious electorate), nor were they required to exhaust their energies in sweeping away the anachronisms which littered the landscape of history. Here they were able to translate their ideas into institutions. This is a major difference between the New and the Old World Enlightenments—that in America the people, not the enlightened monarchs or professional philosophers, were able to get on with the job, and did.

No need, here, to war against feudalism because, except for vestigial remains like primogeniture and entail, which fell almost without a struggle, there was none. No need to topple a ruling class (the exodus of the loyalists had simplified matters here, no doubt), for by Old World standards there was no ruling class, certainly none that was legally entitled to rule or to enjoy special privileges, unless you regard the whole of the white population as in that category. Neither wealth, nor education, nor family could confer privilege in national affairs, only color: under the Constitution adopted in 1788 any free white man could hold the office of President, Justice of the Supreme Court, Secretary of State, or minister, no matter how rich or poor, how devout or agnostic, how learned or ignorant. No need to struggle against the power and pretensions of the military, or the threat of a "standing army"—which was almost an obsession. After the treaty of peace the army stood at 840 men and 46 officers; when Washington took office it was increased to 1,216 men and 57 officers! No need, either, to throw the army open to talent. In France at that time the officer corps consisted of 6,353 nobles and 1,845 commoners and "soldiers of fortune," and in Prussia a few years later there were 700 commoners in an officer corps of 7,100. No wonder a French officer in the American army reported with incredulity that "our inn-keeper was a captain, and there are shoemakers who are colonels"; no wonder Cassius (he was really Aedanus Burke but Cassius sounded more appropriate) assailed the innocuous Society of the Cincinnati as if it were to be a new hereditary nobility that would surely subvert the liberties of America!

No need to struggle against the censorship which everywhere, except perhaps in Holland, hovered like a black cloud over the enterprises of the philosophes—the *Encyclopédie*, for example—and which hurried so many of them into flight: Rousseau to England, Raynal to Holland, Voltaire to Geneva (where they publicly burned his *Philosophical Dictionary*), Priestley to Pennsylvania, Van der Kemp to New York, Madame de Staël to Coppet. No need to repudiate a censorship which condemned the wretched Abbé Dubourg to a lingering death in an iron cage for a harmless squib called *The Chinese Spy* and sentenced to life imprisonment a poor woman who had been caught peddling a copy of Holbach's *Christianity Unmasked*; which in Württemberg jailed the great scholar-statesman Johann Moser (he wrote 266 books) for five years for criticizing the financial irresponsibility of Karl Eugen; which outlawed Tom Paine for the crime of *The Rights of Man* (it went through 21 editions in the United States without doing any perceptible harm); which, after 1789, banned all French books from Russia: and which denied Immanuel Kant the right to publish or lecture on religion. No need for all this, for there was no censorship, or none that mattered. No need to agitate for the end of torture—an end to the spectacle of Calas broken on the wheel or La Barre tortured and burned or a wretched Milanese youth tortured and executed for shouting, in a church, "Long live liberty"—for torture was unknown to American law.

No need to campaign for the secularization of education. It was, by Old World standards, already secularized. One of the purposes of creating public schools in the Bay Colony was to outwit "ye ould deluder Satan," but that maneuver was directed by the secular branch of the community, not the ecclesiastical, or—if it was difficult to make this distinction in the 1640's —that was certainly true during the era of the Enlightenment. No religious tests sifted applicants to colleges and universities (not until 1871 could dissenters attend the universities of Oxford or Cambridge), nor were there religious tests for professors. In the 17th century a Baptist sat in the president's chair at Harvard College, and in the opening days of the 19th century a Unitarian was elected to the Hollis Chair of Divinity (as late as 1862, Cambridge University turned down a professorship of American history on the ground that the incumbent might be a Unitarian!). The charter of the College of Rhode Island, established especially for the proper training of Baptists, provided that "all members shall forever enjoy free, absolute, and uninterrupted liberty of conscience" and that the board of trustees should include Anglicans, Congregationalists, and Quakers. So, too, trustees of the new college of Philadelphia included Presbyterians and Anglicans, as well as Quakers, and Franklin, who was a deist, served as the first president of the board. Jefferson's new University of Virginia was based on "the illimitable freedom of the human mind." "Here" he wrote, "we are not afraid to follow truth wherever it may lead, nor to tolerate any error as long as reason is left free to combat it." And, needless to say, where the state universities of the Old World faithfully reflected the established religion, the new American state universities which emerged, on paper at least, in the 1780's, embraced as a matter of course the principle of religious freedom for students and faculty alike.

Everywhere in the Old World the church shared with the crown responsibility for the minds and souls of the people, and we know from the heated debates on the modification of the Test Acts throughout much of the 18th century how sacred this connection was assumed to be, and how pernicious any slightest rent in the seamless web of conformity. Rich, formidable, and intractable, the church controlled almost everything it touched, and there was not much that it did not touch. It guarded the gates of universities and would not permit dissenters to enter; it censored literature and scholarship and science, too: the Sorbonne rejected the doctrines of William Harvey and Salamanca those of Newton, and in Denmark the church fought some of the medical reforms of Dr. Struensee—even when he was prime minister—on the ground that they were sacrilegious. It sat on the benches of the courts, dispensed justice and injustice, and hanged Pastor Rochette for conducting Protestant services, and it would no more tolerate Catholic teachers than Catholic priests in Ireland. It owned half the soil of Tuscany, Portugal, and Belgium and exercised political as well as ecclesiastical jurisdiction over vast areas of Italy and Spain. And it exiled 18,000 Protestants from the archbishopric of Salzburg, 1,200 of whom eventually found refuge in Georgia.

Nowhere in the American colonies or states was there an established church that enjoyed power even remotely comparable to that enjoyed by establishments almost everywhere in Europe. What Crèvecoeur observed in the third of his letters was generally true, that:

> persecution, religious pride, contradiction, are the food of what the world commonly calls religion. These motives have ceased here. Zeal in Europe is confined; here it evaporates in the great distance it has to travel. There it is a grain of power enclosed; here it burns away in the open air and consumes without effect.

An Isaac Backus might protest this genial view of the American religious scene. The interesting thing—interesting assuredly to Old World observers —is that he did, and that in his famous confrontation with John Adams on religious liberty, it was Adams who was embarrassed, and that in the end the greatest champion of religious liberty in New England since Roger Williams was able to accept the religious provisions (or nonprovisions) of both the Massachusetts and the United States Constitutions.

Consider the familiar, even hackneyed, story of the struggle for religious freedom in Virginia. There the Anglican establishment was as powerful, as rich, and as socially distinguished as anywhere else in the United States —or so it seemed. In 1776, however, Mason's Bill of Rights established religious freedom in the new state, and in 1779 the church was quietly disestablished, almost without a furor. That same year Jefferson (himself a formal though not precisely a devout Anglican) prepared a bill to separate church and state. Patrick Henry attempted to circumvent the proposal by the clever stratagem of providing aid for all denominations, and the struggle was on. With his famous "Remonstrance" Madison rallied support to the principle of complete separation, and in 1785 and 1786 Jefferson's statute of religious liberty was triumphantly enacted. Jefferson described the campaign for separation of church and state as "the severest contest in which I have ever been engaged." If that were indeed true, it would cast a roseate glow on the American scene. For no one in Virginia —or elsewhere in America—went to the stake for his faith (the Reverend Jonathan Boucher was burned in effigy, but not for his religious views!); none was forced to flee to a more hospitable climate, none was ousted from his pulpit or his university, none was subject to censorship or even to contumely. We cannot but wonder what Voltaire would have thought of Jefferson's observation, or any one of the scores of philosophes who wore out their lives, and sometimes lost them, in a vain struggle to overthrow the *infâme*.

4

The institutionalization of Enlightment principles was political and constitutional. We take that for granted but the Old World could not: statesmen there had to content themselves with Pope's admonition

> For forms of government let fools contest,
> What e'er is best administered is best.

They made important contributions to administrative reform, but few to politics and none to constitutionalism. The constitutions which glimmer fitfully in the literature of the day are daydreams of the philosophes: Rousseau's model constitutions for Corsica and Poland, for example, or the blanket *Code de la Nature* of Morelly (the poor fellow has no other name, and perhaps no existence), or the Abbé Mably's constitution for Poland and for American states too—he even claimed credit for the constitution of Massachusetts—or G. E. Lamprecht's curious design for an ideal government for Prussia which assigned to the monarch responsibility for "making the citizens in every regard more well behaved, healthier, wiser, richer and more secure," or von Haller's *Usong* with its wonderful summary of the duties of an enlightened despot. When it came to making real constitutions, however, Europe had little to show. The French tried 13 which did not work; the Americans made do with one, which did.

There is a paradox here, one to which we are so accustomed that we scarcely appreciate it. Surely anyone looking objectively at the world of the 18th century might have concluded that although Americans had a certain shrewdness about local government, they did not have true political sophistication, not the kind needed for creating a nation or solving those intractable problems which for more than two millenia had been glaring upon mankind. Such talent, surely, was to be found in the busy haunts of men—the courts, the capitals, the great universities and academies—of the Old World, not in some pastoral paradise such as Crèvecoeur had imagined. But that is not the way it turned out. It was, in the end, Americans who proved sophisticated. How fascinating that the people most deeply committed to the principle of the supremacy of law over man should be perhaps the only one where the principle was not really needed, and that the people most profoundly suspicious of power in government should be perhaps the only one whose leaders seemed immune to the corruptions of power.

I speak, of course, in terms of the 18th century.

How paradoxical, too, that from a society of three million, with a body politic of perhaps half a million, spread thin over an immense territory, with no populous cities, no great centers of learning, and no tradition of high politics, should come in one generation the most distinguished galaxy of statesmen to be found anywhere in that century or, perhaps, since. You will remember that Jefferson made precisely this point in *Notes on the State of Virginia*, where he asserts with the straightest of faces that on the basis of population France should have eight Washingtons and eight Franklins. (Was it modesty that kept him from adding eight Jeffersons, too, or the realization that this would occur to all his readers?) And how astonishing, too—indeed so providential that perhaps only a Parson Weems could do it justice—that the generation which presided over the birth of the Republic stayed on to direct its destinies for another 50 years!

"Politics is the divine science, after all," wrote John Adams, who somehow never mastered it, and the author of *Notes on Virginia*, though he shunned the term divine, nevertheless agreed that:

the creation of a proper political system was the whole object of the revolution, for should a bad government be instituted for us in the future, it would have been as well to have accepted at first the bad one offered to us from beyond the water.

"Creation" is perhaps the most interesting word here—for if American political principles were not new, the mechanisms were. What impresses us—particularly now in our current phase of intellectual impotence and political sterility—is precisely the resourcefulness, the fecundity, the creative energy of that generation. As Tom Paine observed in *The Rights of Man,*

the case and circumstances of America present themselves as in the beginning of a world.... We have no occasion to roam for information into the obscure fields of antiquity, nor hazard ourselves upon conjecture. We are brought at once to the point of seeing government begin, as if we had lived in the beginning of time.

What the Americans of the Revolutionary generation did is too familiar to justify rehearsal. What they did was to put on the road to solution almost all those great problems which had bemused and perplexed political thinkers from ancient times. They turned to the enduring problem of the origin and authority of government, and announced that government derived its just powers from the consent of the governed, who had the right, when they wished, to institute new governments. And they proceeded to institutionalize that great principle in the constitutional convention—it was almost the private invention of John Adams. They turned to the even more difficult problem of placing limits on power and undertook to solve it by a complex network of institutions and mechanisms: the written constitution as a body of "supreme law"; bills of rights which for the first time guaranteed substantive as well as procedural rights; separation of powers —separation rather than the British "balance"—and an elaborate scheme of internal checks and balances, including that of nation and state; and— after some experimentation—judicial review. They took the idea of federalism, which had never worked successfully, solved its most complex problem of the distribution of powers, and its most importunate problem of sanctions, and created the first successful and enduring federal government. The British Empire had been wrecked on the rocks of colonialism. Americans, with their independence, inherited colonies as large as the original 13 states; they disposed of their colonial problem by the simple device—which no one had thought of since the days of the Greek city-states—of doing away with colonies altogether and calling them states. They contrived instruments and devices for making these institutions work: an incomparably broader suffrage than obtained anywhere else in the western world, and a broader participation in community affairs, too, than in any other communities except possibly Iceland and some of the smaller Swiss cantons. Add atop this an elected chief executive, a really independent judiciary— something no European state could boast—and, perhaps most original of all, political parties much more responsive and effective than the Hats and Caps of Sweden or the Whigs and Tories, the factions and cliques of British politics.

I have already mentioned some other remarkable innovations, or creations, quite as important in their way as the political or constitutional: the establishment of true freedom of the press; the achievement of a broader literacy than was to be found elsewhere in the western world, and with it provision for public education which reached a larger proportion of the population than it did elsewhere; and finally a growth of social and economic equality beyond anything to be found in the Old World.

This achievement dramatizes the most tragic failure of the American Enlightenment: the failure to put Negro slavery on the road to extinction. The failure was not—I know there are some who will disagree with this —a failure of the American Enlightenment but rather a failure of Romanticism. But that is another story.

The frustration of the bright hopes of a Jefferson, a Rush, a Benezet, a Jay, and so many others, does in turn dramatize one striking feature of the American Enlightenment which again is taken for granted or misinterpreted: that it did not collapse into revolution or reaction. There was no American Thermidor, not even in the philosophical and intellectual arena. Loyalists who might have led such a reaction either had left or had returned reconciled; the hard times of the confederation period did not lead to disillusionment with the achievements of the war, or to a repudiation of the great advances in politics, humanitarianism, and reform. At a time when the French were turning to Napoleon the Americans turned to Jefferson, and the Jeffersonian era outlasted the Napoleonic.

The passion and the zeal for institutionalization extended even to the realm of moral philosophy. Consider the 18th-century obsession with happiness. Like the song of the whippoorwill echoes in the literature of every nation felicity, felicity, felicity. The French immersed themselves in it— Mauzi lists almost a thousand novels, poems, and dramas on the theme in his study of happiness in 18th-century France. The Germans analyzed it philosophically. The Italians wrote operas about it. Down in Modena the great historian Muratori wrote a two-volume treatise, *De la Felicité*. In Altona young Dr. Struensee published a *Zeitschrift für Nutzen und Vergnügen*, and it was clear that it was the *Vergnügen* that most interested him. And the author of the *Essay on Man* hailed happiness as:

> ...our being's end and aim,
> Good, pleasure, ease, content, whate'er thy name,
> That something still which prompts th'eternal sigh
> For which we bear to live, and dare to die.

Even in America it was not just romantics like Jefferson and Tom Paine and Joel Barlow who invoked it but pious parsons like Dr. Samuel Johnson of King's College and stout realists like John Adams and George Washington. Listen to the exultant words that Dr. Johnson puts into the mouth of his angel Raphael:

How exquisitely is the whole system of nature about you fitted to every one of your necessities, occasions and conveniences! How agreeably is your sight feasted with the variety of colors, your hearing with pleasing sounds, your smelling with grateful odors, and your taste with delicious morsels. In short: how exactly is everything fitted to all the purposes of your subsistence, comfort and delight. And lastly what a wonderful machine is that which you carry about you by which you are enabled to have commerce one with another.

John Adams, who rarely agreed with anyone, wrote in 1776 that "upon this point all speculative politicians will agree, that the happiness of society is the end of government, as all divines and moral philosophers will agree that the happiness of the individual is the end of man." Washington referred to happiness or felicity five times in the central paragraph of his Circular to the States of 1783, and Crèvecoeur no less than 13 times in the second of his *Letters*. The Virginia Bill of Rights guaranteed the right not only to pursue but to obtain happiness. Jefferson did not go quite that far, but he went to immortality. It was a theme he returned to again and again —remember that lovely line in the first inaugural which invokes the blessings of "Providence, which by all its dispensations proves that it delights in the happiness of man here, and his greater happiness hereafter." I like best his letter to Maria Cosway, over in France, with whom he conducted what by modern standards was a very low-key flirtation, congratulating her on the birth of a daughter. "They tell me *que vouz allez faire un enfant....* You may make children there, but this is the country to transplant them to. There is no comparison between the sum of happiness enjoyed there and here."

The whole point of this is that happiness was not just an ideal or a theory, it was a fact, and if it was not, it *ought* to be. It was rooted in material abundance: as Chastellux wrote, "America has no poor." It was protected by a benign social and political order: as Crèvecoeur wrote: "We have no wars to devastate our fields; our religion does not oppress the cultivators; we are strangers to feudal institutions; our laws are simple and just." It was sustained by universal, or almost universal, enlightenment: as Jefferson wrote of education, "No other sure foundation can be devised for the preservation of freedom and happiness."

But all this was not enough: there should be legal guarantees, too. Mason had put happiness into the Virginia Bill of Rights, and John Adams wrote it five times into the Massachusetts constitution. Soon it became a regular feature of state constitutions. Altogether from the Revolution to the beginning of this century there were some 120 state constitutions. Howard Mumford Jones has calculated for our edification that about two-thirds provided some guarantee of happiness, and that most of these guarantee the right not only to pursue but to obtain happiness. If only our local authorities would realize that the right to obtain happiness is constitutionally secured, they could put an end to all the tiresome confrontations with the young by the simple device of granting them their constitutional rights.

5

There were two large philosophical concepts of the Enlightenment—preoccupations even—which did not so much lend themselves to institutionalization as suffuse and vindicate such institutionalization in the New World. One was deeply rooted in European thought, the other was largely a product of American experience. I refer to the doctrine of progress and to the philosophy of history as prospective rather than retrospective.

Consider first the idea of progress, that *ignis fatuus* which glimmered before the fascinated gaze of so many of the philosophes of the Old World and which was so speedily and so tragically juxtaposed with its own repudiation, as it were, in the drama of a Condorcet clutching the *Equisse* (metaphorically at least) as he took his own life, and of the confrontation, just two months later, between Coffinhal and Lavoisier: "The Republic has no need of savants" (if it is not literally true, it is *ben trovato*). How the philosophes rejoiced in the discomfiture of the ancients by the moderns, in the spread of the empire of reason, in the reinforcements from China, in the ability of Diderot to overcome every obstacle and bring the *Encyclopédie* to a triumphant conclusion, in the expulsion of the Jesuits, in the growth of prosperity and, above all, of population, that most visible, that most irrefutable, argument for progress.

Americans, too, embraced the doctrine of progress, but they produced no analytical treatises, no formal programs, no utopian models. That is not because they were not conscious of progress, but because they took it for granted. Well might they affirm that all their reports on America were studies in progress, all their political programs manifestations of progress, all their statistics demonstrations of progress, and that as for utopian romances, what was America herself but a utopian romance? The formal literature which Americans produced on progress is negligible, but the idea of progress suffuses much of the writing of the day, and shines forth with special radiance from the writings of Franklin, Jefferson, Tom Paine, Joel Barlow, Dr. Rush, even from the writings of stout conservatives like Ezra Stiles and Timothy Dwight.

How different the notion of progress in the Old World and the New! It was, we are tempted to say, a different concept masquerading under the same name. The ultimate goal is doubtless the same on both sides of the Atlantic (though even that can be questioned)—the triumph of reason and the achievement of happiness—but the meaning of these terms received very different readings.

In the Old World (these generalizations are of course wholly lacking in cautious discrimination) progress meant chiefly improvement in the arts, learning, and science, and the gradual refinement of manners and perhaps even of morals. Thus at the very beginning of the great inquiry, d'Alembert's *Preliminary Discourse* to the *Encyclopédie* refers to "progress of the mind," "philosophy," "erudition and belles lettres," "the attitude toward human knowledge," and so forth. And here, 40 years later, is Dodson's edition of the *Encyclopaedia*—which, unlike the *Encyclopédie*, was published in America—somehow equating civilization with "magnificent buildings, noble statues, paintings expressive of life and passion, and poems." No suggestion here (though the article appeared under the rubric "Society") that the well-being of the masses, the amelioration of slavery or of the penal code, or the reign of peace were involved in progress, and no wonder, for in the end the author embraces the cyclical theory of history and thus disposes of progress altogether.

Progress, in the Old World, was a class concept, too, something the philosophes could formulate and the nobility and the intellectuals enjoy. Even the most ardent critics of the establishment—church or state—confessed little interest in the lot of the lower classes, everywhere the overwhelming majority of the population; not Voltaire or Montesquieu, not Raynal or Rousseau, not Lessing or Kant or von Haller or Goethe. Struensee perhaps in Denmark, and Beccaria in Milan and Tom Paine and Priestley in England, but they fled to America. No, as Immanuel Kant observed in his *Strife of the Faculties*, progress, "if it is to come, must come from above, not by the movement of things from the bottom to the top, but by the movement from the top to the bottom. . . . to expect to train men who can improve themselves by means of education of the youth in intellectual and moral culture, is hardly to be hoped for." Nor did the philosophes look to the community, or the body politic, to achieve social progress. After all, except in England, Sweden, and some of the Swiss cantons, there was, strictly speaking, no body politic—not, certainly, as there was in Massachusetts or in Pennsylvania. Progress was something to be achieved through enlightened despots, or members of royal academies, or through the philosophes themselves, not through the people.

How different the American conception of progress here: to summarize a complex affair, progress was not a matter of cultural refinement but of material welfare and of freedom, a matter of health, wealth, education, and freedom to worship, to marry, to move about from region to region, from profession to profession. It was—and long remained—a matter of milk for the children, meat on the table, a well-built house and a well-filled woodshed, cattle and sheep in the pastures and hay in the barn,

> Where every farmer reigns a little king
> Where all to comfort, none to danger rise,
> Where pride finds few, but nature all supplies
> Where peace and sweet civility are seen. . . .
> Where. . . . round me rise
> A central school house, dress'd in modest guise!
> Where every child for useful life prepares,
> To business molded ere he knows its cares:
> In worth matures, to independence grows,
> And twines the civic garland o'er his brows
>
> TIMOTHY DWIGHT, *Greenfield Hill* (1794)

Franklin and Paine, characteristically American both of them, will serve as archetypes of philosophers of progress. No one more confident of progress than Franklin, who thought of it, always, in practical terms. It meant better lighting, paved streets, a circulating library, an efficient stove and an efficient government, peace with the Indians. It meant the Junto library and the College of Philadelphia and the American Philosophical Society. It meant the Albany Plan of Union and the Articles of Confederation and the Constitution. It meant moral progress, to be sure, but that too was a practical ideal, whether regulated by the famous score box with the round dozen moral virtues that were to be cultivated by "habitude," or by new standards of international relations. Franklin did not aim at perfection: he did not suppose that Pennsylvania was Utopia, but he tried to make it less class ridden, less corrupt, less barbarous in its treatment of the Indian, and he succeeded.

There is no formal treatise on progress in the American literature of this era, but *The Rights of Man* comes closer to this than anything else, closer, certainly, than Joel Barlow's *Columbiad,* which purports to unfold (in 6,000 lines) before the enraptured gaze of Columbus a vision of the progress which would eventually encompass the world. Tom Paine had not only grand ideas about the future of man and civilization, but a specific program for the advancement of material well-being and social justice. "Establish the rights of man," he wrote,

Enthrone equality, form a good constitution, let there be no privileges, no distinctions

of birth, no monopolies; make safe the liberty of industry and of trade, the equal distribution of family inheritance, publicity of administration, freedom of the press. These
things established you will be assured of good laws.

These things established you will be sure of progress.

There was one test of progress on which philosophers, economists, and
statesmen on both sides of the ocean were agreed; that was the test of
population. "I am constantly astonished," wrote Rousseau, "that people
should fail to recognize . . . a sign that is so simple. What is the purpose of
political association? It is the preservation of prosperity of its members.
And what is the most certain sign that they are prospering? It is the number and increase of population." Or as Raynal put it, "the point is not to
multiply in order to make men happy, it is sufficient to make them happy
that they should multiply."

Here was, indeed, the incontrovertible test, and by this test the Old
World did badly. There were improvements, to be sure, in the second
half of the century, thanks to the potato, thanks to inoculation. But during
the 18th century population over large areas of Europe—Spain, Portugal,
and many of the Italian states—barely held its own. In Paris—the figures
are from Buffon—10,000 out of 24,000 babies died during their first five
years. In London the figure was even higher, and the magisterial Dr. Price
presented figures which proved that there were 135 deaths for every 100
births in Berlin and no less than 169 deaths per 100 births in prosperous
Amsterdam. Everywhere the story was the same—five out of 12 children
born in the great cities died before they reached the age of five! During
the third quarter of the century Copenhagen lost population three years
out of every four, and even the population of rural Jutland declined. Elsewhere the prospect was not so bleak. Sweden increased its population by
two-thirds during the century; Britain (including Ireland), Hungary, Bo-
hemia, and Finland almost doubled.

But look at America. Everywhere from Maine to Georgia the story was
the same: Americans were obeying the Biblical injunction to multiply
and replenish the earth. There population doubled not in a century but
every 20 or 25 years—the estimates vary, but only within these limits.
Franklin demonstrated that the population of Pennsylvania doubled in 20
years, Jefferson that the population of Virginia, including slaves, doubled
in 27 years; Jeremy Belknap recorded that, notwithstanding the ravages of
the war, the population of New Hampshire more than doubled between
1770 and 1790. Soon, what with Dr. Rush's *Medical Inquiries*, and Benjamin Smith Barton's observations on the progress of population, and Dr.
William Currie's *Historical Account of the Climates and Diseases of the*

United States, and Noah Webster's *Brief History of Epidemic and Pestilential Diseases,* and the speculations of historians like Samuel Williams and Hugh Williamson, American scientists were almost as busy with demography as is the Sixième Section today though—consider the Reverend Edward Wigglesworth's confident prediction of a population of 1,280,000,000 by the year 2000—not quite as cautious. And not only did population double every quarter century, but the whole of America was a kind of fountain of youth, where men and women lived, if not forever, at least well past the span allotted them by the Bible. It was a product of a salubrious climate, to be sure, but climate was more than physical environment, more than abundance of land and variety of soil and fecundity of animal life; it was a product of the social system where mothers could stay home and nurse their babies: it was the product of a religious system where the church did not wrest tithes out of an impoverished peasantry; it was the product of a benevolent political system which encouraged freedom; it was a product of simplicity, innocence, and purity of morals. None put this better than Hugh Williamson, whose *History of North Carolina* meets most of the qualifications of modern cultural anthropology:

The very consciousness of being free excites a spirit of enterprise and gives a spring to the intellectual faculties. If I could speak of our liberties as we speak of the climate and face of the country; if I could speak of their duration as we speak of things that are permanent in nature: I should venture with confidence to predict that in the scale of science the American states, in a few ages, would not shrink from a comparison with the Grecian republics, or any other people recorded in history.

6

Finally, out of all this emerged what may be the one original contribution of Americans to the philosophy, as distinct from the practices, of the Enlightenment: a new theory of history or, perhaps, we should say a new theory about history. History occupied a central position in the thinking of the Founding Fathers, but the history which they cultivated was really a branch of moral philosophy. It was, in the familiar phrase of Bolingbroke, philosophy teaching by examples. Yet this moralistic interpretation of history was not without grave perils, for what was it, after all, that the examples taught? They taught—we can read it in that ambitious historical hodgepodge, *A Defence of the Constitutions of Government of the United States of America . . .* —that men and governments were everywhere and at all times the same; that men were creatures of interest, greed, ambition, and vanity; and that governments tended everywhere to tyranny. And what reason was there to suppose that the new United States would be exempt from the laws of history? The moral lessons which Adams and most of his associates drew from this contemplation of the past was that the supreme task of statesmanship (one itself doomed to eventual frustration) was to contrive checks and balances which might thwart the innate propensities of all men to corruption and of all governments to tyranny.

Jefferson, for one, refused to embrace this dusty answer to the hopes of men. He had read the same histories as had John Adams and found in them the same moral lessons. But he was not prepared to admit that these applied inexorably to the American experiment. On the central issue of the applicability of the historical past to America, he challenged almost the whole of Enlightenment historical thought, and his challenge was but another example of that fascinating blend of the romantic with the classical which makes him the most interesting man of his age. "I like the dreams of the future," he said, "better than the history of the past."

Where Adams saw history as retrospective, Jefferson saw it as prospective. Where Adams took for granted that Americans were prisoners of the past, doomed forever to repeat its follies and errors, Jefferson was confident that man was not the prisoner of history but might triumph over it. Nor was this merely a sentimental hope; as with everything in Jefferson, it was based on what he thought scientific premises. The past need not control the history of America, because, as Jefferson wrote to Dr. Priestley a few weeks after he had assumed the Presidency, "This whole chapter in the history of man is new." For the first time nature was everywhere benevolent and government beneficent. For the first time men were emancipated from the tyrannies and superstitions which had heretofore held them in thrall. For the first time science was available to solve the material problems and education to solve the social and moral problems which had throughout history bedeviled mankind. And for the first time geographical isolation offered immunity from those insensate wars which had for thousands of years made a shambles of the brightest hopes of mankind. The past belonged to the Old World, but the future belonged to America.

★ ★ ★

We do not commonly think of James Monroe as a spokesman for the Enlightenment, and I have managed so far without invoking his name. Yet he was a product of the same Virginia, the same William and Mary, the same revolutionary fervor, that nourished Jefferson, and he lived all his life in the shadow of Monticello. Let me conclude with a passage from his first inaugural address, which came almost at the close of the American Enlightenment, a passage which sums up much of the thinking of that Enlightenment, and which has now, alas, an elegiac quality:

Never did a government commence under auspices so favorable, nor ever was success so complete. If we look to the history of other nations, ancient or modern, we find no example of a growth so rapid, so gigantic, of a people so prosperous, and happy. In contemplating what we have still to perform, the heart of every citizen must expand with joy when he reflects how near our government has approached to perfection: that in respect to it we have no essential improvement to make: that the great object is to preserve it in the essential principles and features which characterize it, and that that is to be done by preserving the virtue and enlightening the minds of the people.

After earning B.A. and Ph.D. degrees from the University of London, Caroline Robbins came to the United States as a Riggs fellow in history at the University of Michigan and taught at Western Reserve University. In 1929 Miss Robbins joined the faculty of Bryn Mawr College, becoming chairman of the history department in 1957 and Marjorie Walter Goodhart Professor in 1960. Upon her retirement in 1971 she was named Professor Emeritus and was honored with an award for distinguished teaching. She has also been a visiting professor at the University of Michigan, the University of Delaware, the University of Pennsylvania, Haverford College, and Hunter College.

A frequent contributor of articles on England and the United States during the Revolutionary era to professional journals, Miss Robbins was editor of The Diary of John Milward, Esq., Member of Parliament for Derbyshire, September, 1666 to May, 1668 *(1938),* Two English Republican Tracts *(1969),* Plato Redivivus, or a Dialogue concerning Government by Henry Neville *(1969), and* An Essay upon the Constitution of the Roman Government by Walter Moyle *(1969) and is author of* The Eighteenth-Century Commonwealthman *(1959), for which she won the Herbert Baxter Adams Prize. She was a member of the Council of the Institute of Early American History and Culture from 1964 to 1967 and has been President of the Conference of British Studies since 1971. She holds a Doctor of Laws degree from Smith College and in 1971 received a Doctor of Letters degree from Wilson College. Since 1967 Miss Robbins has been chairman of the papers of William Penn project.*

THE TWO PAPERS that follow and the commentaries on them
will explore the roots of that republicanism which is so central
to the mentality of the people of the Revolutionary generation.
That it was a term that transcended politics but was infused
with a moral outlook is one of the innovative contributions that
our next speaker has made to the history of ideas. And she
has also made it abundantly clear that it was not a notion
monopolized on this side of the water. It is fair to say that
Caroline Robbins' *The Eighteenth-Century Commonwealthman*,
published some dozen years ago, has already become a classic,
providing the first full-dress treatment of the relevance of radical English thought to Revolutionary America, an area which
Bernard Bailyn and Gordon Wood have subsequently explored
for this side of the ocean with signal illumination.

European Republicanism
in the Century and a Half
Before 1776

CAROLINE ROBBINS

THE DECLARATION OF INDEPENDENCE was not a republican document. Its
eloquent words were prompted by conviction of mistreatment, of just
claims ignored, and a belief—nourished by the abundance and opportunity
of a new world—in the possibility of achieving life, liberty, and the pursuit of happiness in these United States. What John Adams and others
called "revolution principles"[1] had often been explained and could boast
an ancient tradition. For those acknowledging their validity, resistance to
all that violated the natural rights of man was lawful. Liberty could be
defended against tyrants, kings who forsook the customs of the constitution, princes who professed and imposed heretical doctrines, rulers who
failed to protect against disorder at home and invaders from abroad. With
such ideas in mind, the Dutch in 1581 had declared themselves freed from

allegiance to Philip II of Spain. He had both infringed ancient privileges and ignored just remonstrances. They therefore joined their several provinces in a union expedient for the common good.[2]

During the turmoils of the 16th and 17th centuries, Catholic and Protestant alike justified rebellion and even tyrannicide. Proponents of the mythical Gothic freedom of the feudal world tangled with the growing sovereignty of Renaissance theory. The problem of obedience became infinitely more complex than adherence to the old formula of rendering unto Caesar or of fulfilling contractual duty in community or fief. Vigorous articulation of the obligations of submission were countered by unequivocal expressions of resistance rights. Religion, history, law and expediency were studied for arguments. Great social and constitutional changes were taking place, and men anxiously examined the best means of ensuring stability and prosperity. In the explosion of political controversy the new printing presses were kept busy.

But an American in 1765 or 1776 had no need to have recourse to European writing. James Wilson in May 1776 declared: "In Magna Charta, there is a Clause, which authorises the People to seize the K[ing]'s Castles, and opposes his Arms when he exceeds his duty."[3] English republicans afforded ample material for a justification of rebellion. Milton defended the execution of Charles I; Sidney maintained that everyman might kill a tyrant, that nothing in the nature of monarchy obliged nations to bear its exorbitances when it degenerated into tyranny. The rebellion of a whole nation, he declared, could not be called a rebellion.[4] Even less intransigent Englishmen were inclined to look on the possibility of resistance as a concomitant of the freedom they enjoyed. The Seven Bishops opposed James's illegal demands in 1688. John Somers in 1689, when drafting the indictment of James II and the Declaration of Rights to be offered to William and Mary for their endorsement, was said to have had the Dutch declaration of 1581 by his side. Lord Hardwicke believed that in a free country even violent expression of opposition must be seriously considered by those in authority. Sir William Blackstone conceded a natural right to defend a personal interest. Rebellion was widely recognized as one of the cherished rights of Englishmen.[5] To resist abuse of government was, wrote Thomas Gordon, to assist government.[6] "Rebellion to Tyrants is Obedience to God" was another saying suggested as part of the seal of the new United States.

There were also believers in the divine rights of authority and in the absolute submission required to it. Their debates with opponents over the extent of obedience and arguments about the proper way to defend liberty present far fewer and less complex problems than those raised by any consideration of the republican form of government. The word "republic" about the year 1780 was applied to three contemporary confederacies, a number of city-states, and even to three monarchical regimes. Within the preceding 150 years there had been experiments in establishing or setting up conditions for new republics. All failed. Uprisings against constituted authority or battles between rival claimants were not generally republican in design. Masaniello led in the mid-17th century what was briefly a triumphal attack on the Spanish rulers of Naples, but in the moment of victory proclaimed himself, a fisherman, king.

Concepts of republicanism in the third quarter of the 18th century were affected by a number of considerations, among them the nature of contemporary republics or those attempted in the not too distant past and the theory stimulated by the existence of long-lived republics or the failure of recent experiments. As always in searching for definitions in politics, men looked to the writers of the Renaissance and further back to that "ancient prudence" which had contributed to the inspiration of its secular philosophies. In various investigations the conditions under which republics had flourished or declined were carefully scrutinized.

The word "republic" can be used simply to designate a state or commonwealth. The *Oxford English Dictionary* also defines a republic as a state in which government is carried on, nominally or in fact, by the people or by their elected representatives, a society of persons or animals with equality between members. Webster omits the animals and defines a republic as a state in which the sovereign power is in the body of the people. In addition, he notes that the term has been variously applied to ancient city-states, the Roman Republic, the Swiss Confederation, and oligarchies like Venice.

Earlier definitions were not very different. The Encyclopedists[7] of the 18th century listed two kinds of republic: the federation, such as the United Provinces, and the small city-state, often lacking anything of the popular in composition. The idea of federal union as a means of achieving peaceful coexistence among large political entities was examined by men like Andrew Fletcher during the negotiations over the coming together of English and Scottish Parliaments[8] and, in midcentury, by David Hume and Montesquieu.[9] Jean Jacques Burlamaqui saw in confederacy the only means by which several small states, too weak to maintain themselves separately against their enemies, could preserve their liberties.[10] Immanuel Kant saw in federation an aid to world peace.[11] Rousseau recommended it to Poland as the only possible remedy for that country's constitutional ills.[12]

David Ramsay, in an oration celebrating independence, declared that republican government with "equal principles" had scarcely been tried and that "the present mode of taking the sense of the people by representatives" was unknown to the ancients.[13] Montesquieu differentiated between those republics with all or nearly all the population concerned in government and those where only a minority were politically privileged.[14] Two centuries before *The Spirit of Laws* was written, Jean Bodin was already remarking that many republics were thought to enjoy an equal government under a rule of law and with the cooperation of all citizens in their affairs. This idea, he wrote, was like a spider's web, glittering, subtle, finely drawn, but of no strength. Equality could not be preserved save perhaps in the coterie of Swiss republics, small, isolated in the mountains, and with a restless, constantly emigrating population.[15]

The difference between "republican" and "democratic" was not always sharply distinguished. The terms were sometimes used interchangeably. Burlamaqui, a native of Geneva, did not mention the word "republic" when discussing different kinds of government but applied the term both to Poland and to Genoa.[16] Frequently, "democracy" meant rule by the multitude, usually resulting in anarchy. By contrast, "republicanism" denoted a regime of law directed by representatives of the people and often achieving considerable stability. Kant emphasized the error of confounding democratic and republican constitutions. Democracy, he thought, was of necessity despotism. Republicanism was the political principle of separating executive from legislative powers.[17] The philosopher's statement could be disputed but undoubtedly represented a widely held opinion. Robert Palmer's admirable description of the changing concept of democracy during Kant's era need not be considered in the present context.

Voicing the nearly unanimous view of American constitution-makers, James Madison declared that no other save a republican form would be reconcilable with the genius of the people of America, the fundamental principles of the Revolution, and that honorable determination animating every votary of freedom to base all politics on a belief in mankind's capacity for self-government. Madison realized the difficulty of describing what was meant by "republic" and felt obliged to do so himself. Were an answer to the question of what were the distinctive characteristics of the term "republican," he wrote, to be sought not by recurring to principles but in the application of the adjective to specific examples, no satisfaction could ever be found. Like John Adams in his *Defence of the Constitutions of Government of the United States of America* (1787),[18] Madison gloomily rehearsed the deficiencies of contemporary republics in his "Of Ancient & Modern

Confederacies" and, later, in *The Federalist*. The United Provinces allowed no particle of the supreme authority to derive from the people. Venice contained a small group of hereditary nobles exercising absolute power. Poland's aristocracy had scarcely any virtue. Only the Commons in England's polity was in any way republican. Madison concluded that the name "republic" could justly be bestowed only upon a government holding all its powers directly or indirectly from the great body of the people and administered by persons holding office for a limited time.[19] Few of the governments described by both men received even a modicum of praise. But a republic of the kind described by Madison was established in America, a republic containing 13 constituent republics. The makers of the Constitution insisted in the earliest as well as later stages that all states in the federal confederacy or union, whatever other variations might be retained, must be republican in form. The advantages of environment, the legacy of a libertarian tradition, and the talents of an exceptionally gifted generation were combined to good purpose. An added dimension was given to the meaning of "republic" by the American experiment in government, a strong federal state, preserving considerable diversity within its union.

The United States was a new creation. The strictures of Adams and Madison on earlier republics were deserved. Yet a study of history and experience afforded valuable lessons which were constantly cited as the discussions proceeded. Adams and Madison were learned but so also were men like Pierce Butler of South Carolina, James Wilson and Gouverneur Morris of Pennsylvania, Alexander Hamilton of New York.[20] Pitfalls to be avoided were noted, British philosophies and political expedients analyzed. The English-speaking world was familiar with theories of covenant and consent: representation had, if overgenerously interpreted, legal dicta to support its role in the new republicanism. The jury and other juridical liberties were recognized rights. A doctrine of the separation of powers put forward in England during the Interregnum had received the somewhat uncritical encomiums of Montesquieu as an excellent preservative of liberty. It especially helped, it was thought, to prevent that corruption which often menaced the well-being of a popular state. Though some Englishmen had advocated voting by ballot and officeholding by fixed rotation, they had not as yet been adopted in England but were long established in republics like Venice, Genoa, and Ragusa. Nor when the union of Scotland and England took place did England adopt the suggestion of a confederated state. The United Provinces and Switzerland set useful precedents. In a larger confederation, the Holy Roman Empire presented a horrible example of what such a state should avoid in the variety and independence of the component parts. Americans were also familiar with the danger to republics of foreign intrigue and intervention. Commercial affairs and their effects on polity could be studied in the history of Venice, Genoa, and Holland.

For writers of popular constitutions, the most difficult problems have consistently been encountered in defining the nature of the executive. To republicans a prime objective was usually the limitation of the power of prince, doge, or general. Some even considered the omission of any official head of state. Over and over again the rise of a strong leader during a national emergency had proved the undoing of republican institutions. The English Republic was ended by Cromwell; the return of the House of Orange in 1672 heralded the eventual end of that republicanism to which in particular the province of Holland was devoted. Yet in critical times decisions were necessary, and thoughtful 18th-century Venetians, for example, sometimes wished for a more powerful executive.

To suggest, as some authors have done, that European experience was irrelevant to the American discussions of a critical period is altogether to underestimate the attention paid to it in Revolutionary America.[21] A writer of a different way of thinking has, indeed, put forward the theory that some Americans tried to relate their situation to "the universal tendencies of republicanism in all ages."[22] Yet in spite of all the winged words on sovereignty of the people, resistance rights, and natural law, it is not easy to find a continuing and consistent republican philosophy between the *Discourses* of Machiavelli and *The Spirit of Laws* of Montesquieu. Sir Thomas More had described a Utopia, Harrington an Oceana, Baxter a Holy Commonwealth, but in none could a firm statement of republicanism, as such, be found. A good deal that was written decried the abuse of power and the oppression of tyrants. A whole shelf of volumes discussed the virtues of the Venetian Republic, and many others dealt with explanations of the rise and fall of ancient republics.

What the Founding Fathers studied was important and what they made of it, peculiarly their own. They were, it seems, more interested in actual historical examples of the workings of constitutions than in theory, as they debated the Articles of Confederation or the Constitution of 1787. On one occasion in that year, Luther Martin of Maryland read to the company passages from Locke, Vattel, Somers, and Priestley. Jean Burlamaqui was more than once quoted on natural law. The opinions of Richard Price and, more frequently, those of Montesquieu were cited.[23] But on the whole it was with reference to the difficulties of German disunion, of the problems raised by the single vote per province in the Netherlands, and of the nature of the Swiss League that delegates discussed their own dilemmas. As always, men sought to bolster arguments with appropriate illustrations. Even so, it is impossible to read their debates without realizing that the lessons of history had been studied. With this in mind and without recurring to the examination of Greek and Roman constitutions also familiar to a classically educated generation, it may be appropriate here to discuss republics as they existed immediately before 1776 and to glance at the material about the theory of republicanism available to Americans in those critical years.

The example perhaps most often recalled by Americans as they worked out their destiny was that of the United Provinces. As Jonathan Austin declared, the situations were similar in many respects.[24] After casting off allegiance to Philip II, the confederacy achieved security, maintained independence in the face of considerable foreign aggression, and became rich by trade and the acquisition of an overseas empire. The Dutch enjoyed liberty of religion, though none but men of the reformed faith could hold office. Since the union, like the American later, bestowed no titles of honor, men enjoyed a certain equality of status. A council of representatives of each of the seven provinces, a secretary, and the grand pensionary of Holland made up a part of the federal government, another being the states-general in which each province, whatever the number of the delegates sent to it, cast but one vote. Decisions by council or states-general were not final until each provincial estate and every one of their free cities had consented. A single adverse vote could prevent implementation of policy. On July 30, 1776, during debates on article 17 of the Articles of Confederation, the Reverend John Witherspoon used the example of the states of Holland to support the statement that every colony was a distinct person. On August 1, debate on the counting by colony or population continuing, Roger Sherman said that Americans, like the Dutch, should vote by states, while Dr. Benjamin Rush, citing Abbé Raynal, declared that, on the contrary, the ruin of the United Provinces had been brought about by the principle of one state, one vote, as well as by the necessity of consulting every constituent part on all matters.[25] The equality in decision-making was regarded as all the more striking since there was great disparity between provinces, Holland being much the richest. That wealth, of course, gave her great influence in public affairs, in spite of the constitution.[26]

Besides illuminating the problems of confederacies, the United Provinces also provided a copybook illustration of the problem of executive power. William the Silent of the principality of Orange in southern France had played a leading role in the 16th-century emancipation of the Dutch from Spanish rule. He was stadholder or governor, an office which could be held by one man in a single province, in several, or in all. In time of war a stadholder general provided the strong leadership entirely lacking in the federal government. The House of Orange was popular in the 17th century with the common people and with the Calvinists. In moments of peril it was accepted by all. But to earnest republicans anxious to maintain states' rights and fearful of the growth of executive power in times of peace, the stadholderate represented a possible menace. Jan van Olden Barneveldt had in the first decades of the 17th century headed the republicans. With his execution in 1619 the Orangists were again in the ascendant. The death of William II in 1650, leaving only an infant heir, made it possible for the Dutch to call an extraordinary assembly, and this abolished the stadholder-ate as a general hereditary office, except in such states as wished individ-ually to elect a governor. For more than 20 years under the leadership of John de Witt and his brother, the United Provinces were, according to the ideas popular in Holland, a true republic. For success, peace was essential. Unfortunately war broke out almost at once and recurred again and again. The de Witts were murdered in 1672. The young William III, already chosen stadholder in some provinces, now took over command of war and foreign policy. In 1747 the electoral process once again gave way to the demand for a hereditary stadholderate. By 1787 the United Provinces were torn by faction and the old republicanism was a thing of the past.[27]

Dutch political literature reflected the contests between supporters of the stadholderate and of a more republican regime. The situation illuminates the natural propensity in society to accept the rule of reformer, general, or politician. The Biblical account of the end of the Hebrew commonwealth was regarded by republicans as a moral story. To them the Jewish federa-tion of tribes, with its individualism and its excellent laws about debt, was admirable. Yet in spite of so wise a system, and in face of the warnings of the Prophet Samuel, the Hebrews had declared: "We will have a king over us that we may be like all nations, that our king may judge us and go out before us and fight our battles."[28] Threatened, like the Hebrews, from without, most of the Dutch were peculiarly susceptible to the ad-vantages of the rule of the stadholders. On the stadholderate and its dis-astrous effect upon republican government both Peter de la Court and Benedict de Spinoza concentrated in their political treatises. *The True In-terest and Political Maxims of the Republic of Holland* first appeared in 1662 during that period when the Holland republicans had prevented the appointment of a general stadholder. Revised a few years later, perhaps with the help of John de Witt himself, de la Court's book appeared in an English translation in London in 1702 just after the death of William III. Its avowed aim was to portray the disadvantages of a stadholder or single ruler. True interest must be sought in the welfare of both governors and governed. Good government should never be dependent upon the virtues or vices of the ruler; it should rather derive from the prosperity of the subjects. The good will of the people was essential. Citadels provided no safeguard for the peace of the state. Interest was paramount; no one "halted of another man's sore." Liberty brought riches and population; republics thrived where these were to be found. Only idle gentry preferred monarchy. Freedom of trade and religion, speedy justice from incorrupt judges, ensured the contentment of the community.

"By the word republic and republican rulers," wrote the author of *The True Interest*, "I mean, not only such a state wherein a certain sovereign assembly hath the right and authority for coming to all resolutions, making of orders and laws, or to break them, as also of requiring obedience or prohibition, but I understand thereby such a state wherein an assembly hath the power to cause all their resolutions . . . to be obeyed." In the Holland of which de la Court wrote, the people in a wider sense had little role in government, yet his book is implicitly popular in tone.[29]

Also sympathetic to the de Witt regime, Spinoza declared himself, even in the tragic year of 1672, a republican. In 1670 he had presented to the world a noble plea for liberty of religion in the *Tractatus* and had raised a storm of protest over its Biblical exegesis. The political treatise was unfinished in 1677 when he died. Enough was left and eventually published to place it firmly in the republican tradition. Politics, he wrote, were a chimera, since in discussing them men normally conceived of their fellows not as they were but as they should be. An acceptance of the limitations as well as of the capacities of Americans helped to form the Constitution of 1787. Spinoza a century before had declared that reason, neighborly love, and the like could not afford sufficient security. Deterrents were essential whatever the government or the virtues of the governed might be. No government could force men to believe or make them love what they hated, nor should it require them to witness against themselves. Commonwealths, if properly constituted on the basis of an understanding of human nature, could be everlasting. Spinoza guessed that one reason for the return of the stadholderate was "not from a useless waste of time in debates, but from the misinformed state of the said dominion and the fewness of its rulers." Those who had political rights were few. Spinoza wrote that all born of citizen parents or on the soil of the country should have the right to vote in the supreme council and to fill public offices. Thus he raised not only the matter of the executive but the important issues of consent and participation in political decisions by the majority of the population.[30]

In the Swiss League all the cantons were republics, the oldest—the forest cantons—having more of the popular in their constitutions. Each part of the confederation, which was formed in the Middle Ages to throw off foreign domination and continued to guarantee mutual security, retained its particular customs and religion. A federal assembly met briefly each year but the union as such lacked a common currency, federal taxation, armed forces, and judiciary. Like Bodin, Madison thought only a peculiar topographical situation held the cantons together. But Sidney and Montesquieu, possibly unaware of occasional civil strife, peasant uprising, and complaints of inequities, had praised the Swiss.[31] Charles Pinckney declared the Swiss and the Dutch the only true republicans. George Mason saw their freedom preserved by their patriotism. James Wilson, more of a realist perhaps, thought the "incumbent pressure" of foreign powers kept the federation united. That vulnerability was often remarked, and the fact of the inequality in size between cantons, in spite of the rule of one state, one vote, was noticed. The sharpest criticism of Switzerland in the Continental Congress debates came from John J. Zubly, a native of St. Gall, who confessed that from his experience he regarded republican government as "little better than a government of Devils." Nonetheless, Switzerland remained—before the revolutionary wars of the late 18th century—secure and peaceful, enjoying a maximum of states' rights, in spite of the slight ties which held the league together.[32]

Geneva was not yet a part of the Swiss Confederation. An oligarchic city republic, it was several times seriously disturbed by the revolts of the underprivileged majority against the ruling burghers and citizens of the republic. A small patrician coterie ruled city and suburbs and was by no means tolerant either of the aspirations of the populace or of any deviation from the religious orthodoxy of the elect. Scarcely a quarter of the inhabitants enjoyed any role whatever in the General Council or in the Councils of Two Hundred and of Twenty. When Voltaire took up residence in Geneva he moved in patrician circles. He had, as his adoption of an aristocratic name reveals, some sympathy for the mores of an upper class. But the situation of the poorer Genevans inspired his *Republican Ideas*, written about 1764 or 1765. In it his concern was concentrated upon the common people. Despotism, he wrote, in whatever form, was always absurd. A rule of law, purged of inequities, was essential to good government, though some regulations—sumptuary laws, for example—were unnecessary. Always the champion of the oppressed in Geneva, Voltaire later began to realize the injustice of excluding from political life most of the inhabitants of a state.[33]

The third of the European confederacies was the Holy Roman Empire, whose inclusion in republican ranks may at first sight seem surprising. Yet writing about 1786, the historian Johan Stephan Pütter compared the confederacy of the New World with the Germanic Empire, which Charles Pinckney was to call an "unwieldy, unmeaning body" and James Wilson "a burlesque on government." This gigantic aggregate of infinitely varied states still had a constitution and federal institutions which, if they had worked, might have made Pütter's comparison less startling. The emperor was elected by a College of Princes, seven, eight, or nine in number at different periods. Save for three years, Habsburg claims on the imperial title remained unchallenged. Few but rulers of such a rich patrimony as the Habsburgs enjoyed could have contested the honor. An imperial ban lacked means of enforcement. A Supreme Court at Wetzlar competed for judicial appeals with the emperor's own Aulic Council at Vienna. A Diet sat at Ratisbon and was composed of the College of Electors, the Bench of Lay and Spiritual Princes, and the Bench of Free Cities. The Diet in theory could collect from the 10 imperial circles the common penny for the payment of imperial forces. Though the emperor was supposed to have some control over these, in practice his influence was confined to what his individual status as a Habsburg conferred. He could confer titles but was obliged to concede those appellations demanded by rulers of states within the empire. Each state within the imperial boundaries managed religious, diplomatic, and warlike activities independently of all others, and even of the emperor himself.[34] Germany afforded an illustration of the dangers of so loose a federation. Yet her universities produced a number of distinguished writers on government and the law of nations, though significantly, perhaps, they did little more than declare the existence of federative republics.[35]

Besides the three confederacies, there were European city-republics of astonishing durability, though by 1776 signs of decay were becoming obvious in many of them. In some, as in Geneva, governing bodies perpetuated themselves. In others, provision for the prevention of tyranny by a single person or corruption by a faction included devices, later widely adopted, like rotation in office and voting by ballot. Earlier town councils or assemblies may well have been attended by most adult males, but by the 17th century, if not before, these excluded the greater number of inhabitants as well as dependent and colonial subjects living in environs and areas acquired by the city. Of these republics Venice was the most famous. Her constitution had been the subject of numerous treatises and many admiring tributes. The public spirit of her ruling merchant aristocracy was praised by Pelatiah Webster. The Dutch kept Spain and France at bay; the Venetians, the Turk. The restrictions upon the doge or duke, the purity of the justice administered, and the wealth amassed over centuries of prosperity gave special luster to Venetian republicanism. English travelers returned to suggest adoption of some of her devices. Amelotte de la Houssaye, French ambassador there during the reign of Louis XIV, is said to have incurred displeasure for the enthusiasm he displayed in a work he later published on the republic.[36]

In the serene Venetian state the doge was elected for life and could act only in consort with ducal councilors, the heads of the judicial system, and the sages who together formed the college or executive responsible for the conduct of affairs. The senate of some 300 members was elected—save for a few ex officio ministers—by the Great Council. Its members served a stated term, so many retiring every year. To this legislative body the college proposed laws. The Great Council, consisting of men over 25 years of age and belonging to a hereditary and long virtually closed caste, was chiefly occupied in electing all officers. Election was elaborate, using ballot, lot, and nominating groups. Persons chosen were finally presented to a general vote. Three juridical bodies and a Council of Ten guarded law and constitution. Scarcely 2,000 nobles were qualified electors by 1700; among these, more than a hundred key offices, besides lesser posts, held for terms of six months or a year, were allotted. Doge, senate, and council in theory represented a mixture of monarchical, aristocratic, and democratic elements, but in the Republic all political activity was narrowly confined. By the 18th century Venice had suffered from war and from diminished political vitality. Among other ways of restoring potency to state policies, men sought to strengthen the limited powers of the doge. Francesco Scipione di Maffei visited England. In his *Consiglio Politico* he accurately reported on the English cabinet system in an attempt to suggest ways of arresting the decline of Venice, under whose protection his native Verona had existed since the 15th century.[37]

Genoa's republic closely resembled that of Venice. Her duke was elected only for a brief term and wore during that time the crown of dependent and often rebellious Corsica. Genoa was threatened and sometimes humiliated by powerful neighbors. She was disturbed not only by Corsican recalcitrants but by the riots of an unprivileged population. For a long while the famous Bank of St. George helped to maintain a good measure of prosperity.[38]

By 1800 most larger and lesser city republics were overwhelmed by the wars of the period. But Biscay enjoyed, at least until 1832, peculiar privileges and the recognition of her republican institutions under the Spanish crown. The mountain republic of San Marino maintained independence. There, said Thomas Dawes in an oration at Boston on March 5, 1781, "every man finds his prosperity in submitting to those laws which defuse equality. There every man feels himself happily liable to be called to the senate or the field." Lucca, Ragusa, and others even less familiar today had until then employed constitutional devices similar to those of Venice. Their wealth also derived from commerce, the enterprise of merchant, seaman, and banker. The two principal dangers to their continued existence were presented by foreign aggression and by domestic discontent. The ruling classes failed to realize a need for adaptation to changing mores and to the demands of an increasingly vocal majority. The strong urban loyalties and public spirit of earlier days had declined and thus failed to provide effective protection against assault from without.[39]

Italian republics, while they flourished, stimulated comment and theory. But even in decline at the end of the 17th and during the 18th century Italy brought forth critics and political theorists. Count Alberto Radicati di Passerano—under the influence of English revolutionary literature brought to his attention most probably by John Molesworth, the English envoy at Turin—became anticlerical in the manner of John Toland and Thomas Chubb and a proponent of king-killing doctrines. He found it best to leave the royal state of Sardinia-Savoy and went first to England and then to Holland, where he died.[40] His work indicates a renewal of Italian political talent, to be found a little later on also in Maffei and, most especially, in the writing of Cesare Beccaria. Chiefly concerned with crime and punishment, Beccaria was also responsible for ensuring a continental circulation to Francis Hutcheson's famous concept of the greatest happiness of the greatest number. Beccaria was quoted on the necessity for fixed, known laws and against the imposition of any unnecessary authority. Throughout the period between Renaissance and Revolution, republicans and all would-be political philosophers continually turned also to the *Discourses* of Machiavelli. In mid-18th century his influence was obvious in the writings of Montesquieu, his most distinguished disciple.[41]

In addition to the "monarchical republics"—England and Poland—noted by Adams, Sweden for a time between 1712 and 1772 also deserved that description. William Tudor on March 5, 1779, referred to Sweden as the bravest, hardiest, freest nation of the north and noted that "in one hour" she was "plunged from the distinguished heights of liberty into abject vassalage." Even by Madison's definition, Sweden had seemed well on the way to true republicanism. She enjoyed a rule of law and free expression of opinion. Vigorous political parties enlivened politics and the peasant farmers in the fourth estate represented an active popular element in the revived parliamentary system. The king exercised no veto, nor did he control the meetings of the Diet and the use of the armed forces. Sweden suffered, as Alexander Hamilton put it, from meddling neighbors, but before the Vasa coup d'etat, it had a limited executive and a representative government in which a fairly wide proportion of the people participated.[42]

Poland, on the other hand, though often listed in the 17th century among the free "Gothic nations" had—as also frequently remarked—an "extremely confused" government, which was headed by an elected king chosen by the nobles on the fields of Warsaw in meetings renowned for their tumultuous character. At those assemblies a single vote could stop implementation of election or policy. More, it was said, voted in Poland than in England, but the Polish upper class, the only politically powerful group, showed no concern about the rest of the population, whose appalling condition exhausted contemporary vocabularies. In Poland also the interference and rivalry of foreign powers like Russia, Turkey, and Prussia was disturbing and eventually brought about partition of the country, a "scene of bloodshed and misery," between her neighbors. The Polish example of elective monarchy was frequently cited as one method of appointing a chief executive to be avoided at all costs.[43]

England, another monarchical republic, contained, according to American commentators, but one republican element in her government. That was, of course, the House of Commons, representing the people and elected in some towns by a wide franchise although in others by one so narrow as not to deserve the term. Even the country franchise exercised by 40-shilling freeholders was less popular than it once was or than its provisions might suggest. Yet in the 18th century any improvement of conditions, widening of the right to vote, modernization of the law courts and procedures, or concessions to the colonies seemed almost impossible to effect. Men attributed this inflexibility to that corruption which had crept in and ruined both the efficiency and the moral purpose of government.

What impressed students of the English Constitution was not only the continuing legal tradition of a rule of law administered, in theory at least, without respect of persons, but also the freedom of speech and of the press. Even Americans after 1776 spoke of the virtues of the British polity. In the Republic as it was fashioned could be found innumerable reminders of

English custom and tradition. The monarchy, limited or balanced by other parts of the constitution and by the possibility of rebellion, to be sure enjoyed more power than most republicans would consider proper. England had not adopted the ballot or rotation in office, had never seriously considered a federal union between the various parts of the British Isles, but over the years she had produced a legal and political literature that emphasized freedom and the doctrine of consent. Lockean doctrines of the equality of the human potential before changed by circumstance, and Shaftesburian optimism, essential for the establishment of a popular system, had revolutionized thinking about the nature and scope of politics. Americans enjoyed a rich heritage of readily available political philosophy.[44]

England had also, less than a century and a half before 1776, been involved in a serious conflict between king and Parliament. At the beginning of the trouble no one, except perhaps Harry Marten, had thought of substituting a republic for the monarchical system. Men were mainly concerned to protect ancient rights from arbitrary rule. Civil war erupted and the king's party was defeated, in large part by the extraordinary army organized by Oliver Cromwell. Political and religious controversy, already wordy, now enormously increased. The rich offerings of the press in the years 1646–60 cannot be briefly surveyed but, in the consideration of a republican tradition, two schools of thought have particular significance. The tracts of the Levellers and the Agreements of the People drawn up in large part by them were not overtly republican in object but obviously voiced a popular doctrine. The second found expression in the treatises written by a gifted group of men who supported the establishment of a commonwealth after the execution of the king in 1649.

The Levellers, among whom John Lilburne was foremost, wished to decentralize government, to limit and regulate all parts of it, to reform the law, and to create a secular state where all could worship as they pleased. The Agreement was not primarily directed against rule by a king: it represented a demand for a written constitution which would become effective only when the people should have voted on it. Excluded from that process were paupers, women, servants, and, for a stated period only, recent opponents in the wars.[45] The first draft of the Agreement was debated in the army council in 1647. Henry Ireton, Cromwell's son-in-law, argued about the most significant point at issue. "Let the question be," he said, "whether a man can be bound to any law that he doth not consent to? and I tell you that he may and ought to be." He noted the obligations of foreign residents. To Ireton's argument Maj. William Rainsborough replied that "an equal voice in election is a just and reasonable thing . . . it ought to be made good." And, he continued, "the chief end of this government is to preserve persons as well as estates, and if any law shall take hold of my person, it is more dear than my estate."[46] For the Levellers the assumptive and non-participatory consent of most contemporary republics and popular states was not enough: consent should be actual and active. For them, as for Montesquieu later, the suffrage was an essential part of the true republican form of government. The people should be represented by persons of their own choice and ruled by laws which they approved. The Levellers had less of the antiquarian and more of the immediate image of English daily life than the commonwealthmen or republicans so-called. They were not, on the whole, bookish. Aware of social inequities, they looked to a more popular solution than, for example, that proposed by James Harrington. They felt, as soldiers have probably felt in all ages, that their efforts in the cause of liberty should be recognized. They briefly excited some enthusiasm in and around London but, lacking organization and with few adherents wise in the ways of English political activity, they failed even briefly to carry out their plans.[47]

One immediate sign of Leveller influence may be discovered in France, where, in the same period, the Fronde uprisings against the unpopular rule of the queen regent and Cardinal Mazarin were disturbing the country. Many interests were involved and some odd alliances effected and broken. Help from abroad was sought by malcontents. In these crosscurrents of disaffection, some of the artisans, small shopkeepers, and craftsmen of Bordeaux implicated themselves, first in protests against a governor they disliked, then in struggles with local legal authorities. Winning an unexpected victory over the latter, they were offered the help of a great noble who thought perhaps to combine popular forces at home with help from the new regime in England—this was after the execution of Charles—to achieve his own ambitions. But Mazarin soon reestablished authority, Condé deserted his allies in Bordeaux, and Cromwell, by now the most powerful of Englishmen, was more willing to bargain with the cardinal than to help the cause of these rebels. The Bordelais were overcome and many were executed.

Under the elms of their city, these French republicans had studied a French translation of the Agreement, *L'Accorde du Peuple*, and issued their own manifesto. No government without the consent of the governed was legal. Taxes bearing harshly upon the poor should be abolished. Oppressions by the higher clergy should be stopped. The peasant should be as free as the prince: when he entered the world he wore neither sabots on his feet nor a saddle on his back. This last was an echo of Sarpi's famous saying, which was to be used again in a slightly variant form by one-eyed Rumbold in his speech before his execution for opposing James II, and still again in a later oration by Thomas Jefferson. The significance of the episode in Bordeaux is greater than the area and numbers concerned or the time consumed. The Levellers, even with the cheers of a London crowd to encourage them, lacked the force to carry out their proposals.[48] Below the surface of political life, and inarticulate except when opportunity seemed to offer, were persons anxious for self-government and prepared to risk much to obtain it. In any study of republicanism, the marketplace and tavern must surely be as important as the conscious expression of political theory by revolutionaries. Unfortunately the discussions of such places are nearly impossible to document. The Bordelais were helpless in face of a powerful minister.

The Agreement of the People can be traced briefly in contemporary France. But the continuing influence of both it and other Leveller manifestos is almost impossible to find elsewhere in political or historical commentary. After the gift of the Thomason tracts to the British Museum in the reign of George III, and the use of some 17th-century tracts by Catharine Macaulay in her *History* at about the same time, there are occasional references to the more radical thought of the English Interregnum. In 1766 in upstate New York discontented tenants called themselves Levellers, but with how much reference to the earlier group I do not know. On both sides of the Atlantic the word "Leveller" was commonly used as a term of abuse. As late as 1776 James Warren dreaded the consequences of a "levelling spirit"[49] in New England and John Adams reported Peter Van Brugh Livingston's dread of the same manifestation. Clinton Rossiter has remarked on the almost total neglect of Lilburne's thought by Americans. That philosophy seems to have become more interesting to them toward the end of the 19th century, when the Agreement was reprinted in the *Old South Leaflets* in Boston, and Charles Firth printed the Clarke Papers containing the army debates in England.[50]

On the other hand, it is safe to state that the republican works of Milton, Ludlow, Harrington, Nedham, Sidney, and Neville were well known and were read by numbers on both sides of the Atlantic. By republicans here is meant those who supported the commonwealth established after the execution of the king. That regime was set up by the Rump Parliament, that is, what remained of the membership after all possible supporters of Charles had been purged from the Long Parliament in December 1648. The Rump also elected annually a council of state and pondered some useful legislation, including the Navigation Act and other acts. It was obliged to find funds to pay the army and navy now fighting with signal success to defend the new republic. No appeal to the people was felt necessary. Nor, had it been made, is it likely that men of the same way of thinking would have been returned by election. The republicans from 1649 to 1653 and again in 1659 were often able and gifted men, but they were not popular and possibly attracted among the crowds less enthusiasm than the Levellers. Montesquieu remarked that they lacked the virtue—public spirit —for a republic, but possibly he might rather have said that in spite of the patriotism of many republicans, they wanted the sense to see that decision and unity of purpose were essential to success. Cromwell displaced them, but even with the fall of his son, they were unable to produce a viable program.

This was a gifted and varied coterie. Men like Milton, Baxter, and Vane cared more for the rule of the good and the wise than for the representation of the people. Others were interested in the relation of property to power and ways to stabilize it. Some were eager for constitutional devices which would prevent tyranny. Others concentrated upon religious liberty. In their treatises, arguments about government continued to attract interest. Their contribution to republicanism is hard to summarize. Advocacy of resistance rights has already been noted. With this went along a realization that government could not be perpetual, that times changed along with clothes, food, and weapons. Men must adapt and so must society. The right to substitute a better government for the old was recognized. They felt that constitutions needed constant supervision and even suggested guardians of the state—Harrington to see his experimental Oceana through its first difficult years, Ludlow for the purpose of preventing backsliding from republican rule. The republicans were not greatly interested in improving representation, though some of their general dicta lent encouragement, as time went on, to those who did. They did not in 1649 adopt the proposals of the Agreement. Nedham and Sidney denied that by "people" they meant any "confused promiscuous body."[51] Harrington's restriction of responsibility to the "elders" greatly narrowed the scope of the franchise in Oceana. Most republicans wished to limit the powers of the executive and perhaps other parts of government by a written constitution. As late as 1680, Henry Neville suggested that four councils elected by but not from Parliament should advise and thus restrict the king in matters of foreign policy, war and peace, armed forces, and expenditure. Nor should the king have a veto upon legislation.[52]

Levellers, republicans, and other revolutionaries agreed that certain legal and ecclesiastical reforms were necessary. They also seem to have developed at about the same time the doctrine of the separation of powers. This was to have a curious history.

Good and free government could only be maintained, the theory went, if the executive and legislative parts of the polity were kept apart. Such a separation would safeguard liberty, lessen the dangers of faction and corruption, and ensure a proper allocation of function. Efficiency would be achieved and the influence of public over private interest encouraged. Officeholders should not also be members of Parliament. The proliferation of such royal servants in the Commons of Charles II led to the nickname "Pensionary Parliament." After the Glorious Revolution an attempt was made to pass a place bill forbidding crown employees to sit, but all that was effectively achieved was to ensure that certain ministers on appointment stood for reelection in their constituency. Separation of powers was a doctrine to which others besides republicans paid tribute. Montesquieu thought he saw in it the secret of English stability. Others regarded it as essentially republican in purpose, and this was the attitude of most Americans. England, even though she did not literally follow its stricter requirements, certainly developed and made popular the concept of a separation of powers. In assessing the English contribution to the theory of republicanism this idea, the notion of representation and consent, and the belief in the possibility or even desirability of alteration in government by force if necessary must all be weighed.[53]

Except for reprints of earlier works, by 1720 republican literature was scarce. The Dutch confederacy was moving away from republicanism. Venice, though as yet not unsuccessful in war, was ruined by war's continuance and never recovered her old prosperity. In 1689 Edmund Ludlow, who had lived in exile at Vevey in Switzerland since 1660, returned to London to find no interest in the establishment of another commonwealth and went back to die in his Swiss refuge. Genoa had been humiliated in 1684 by France, though she still retained her possessions. Criticisms of monarchial policy were rife in France, but these revealed more nostalgia for the feudal liberties of the past than any anticipation of a republican future. Written in the thirties, though not published until 1764, *Considerations on the Government of France* by the Marquis d'Argenson offered a quite drastic plan for revising the constitution in which a democratic and decentralized system would function under a revivified monarchy. Cooperation of king and people might bring liberty to France. Though an advocate of popular participation in government, d'Argenson was not a republican. On the basis of a survey which preceded presentation of his plan, he found little to admire in European systems.[54]

The most influential political writer in mid-18th century was Charles Louis de Secondat, Baron de Montesquieu. Men like Barère were later to think his sympathies republican, but on the whole he seems to have found too many difficulties in the administration of republics to advocate their erection. In the *Persian Letters* he remarked on the problems of discovering what government was most conformable to reason. All had faults. In free states prosperity and population seemed as common as in absolutisms. In the discussion of the grandeur and decline of Rome, possibly inspired by Walter Moyle's *Roman Government*, published while Montesquieu was in England, he contrasted the watchfulness of England over her constitution with Roman carelessness. In *The Spirit of Laws* he defined republics and described confederacies; he also devoted attention to the qualities necessary for the success of the republican form—virtue, love of country, frugality, morality, and equality. He had been influenced by Paolo Mattia Doria and even more by Machiavelli. Federative republics should be all of a kind in any given union or league. All republics should live under a rule of law. All must guard against external foes and the domestic danger afforded by the growth of luxury and vice.[55] In November 1787 Luther Martin gave the Maryland legislature an account of a speech he had delivered earlier against a federal system. During it he declared that delegates had decided that the government advocated by "a Montesquieu and a Price" was impracticable. In spite of Martin, Montesquieu's opinions were favorably viewed by delegates and his name was more frequently quoted than any other.[56]

Republics were various but, as already remarked, always suggested something of the popular in their composition. Some council or body was supposed to represent the people in the republic and help to ensure a rule of known law. The whim of an oligarchy might be harsh and the indifference of an English Parliament hard to tolerate, but neither seemed as tyrannical as the rule of one man, despot or absolute prince. Conditions of officeholding were defined. The elective process, even if too narrowly confined, recognized the principle of choice and rotation in power. Federation allowed liberty for the constituent parts and, generally, security for the union. Republican treatises were little occupied by consideration of inequalities of property and educational opportunity. There was in them more concern to prevent abuse of power than its useful exercise. Rights of free speech and worship, juridical privilege, and equality attracted more attention than the rights and wrongs of social structure and disparate rewards for labor. Men studied the rise and fall of republics, as well as of other governments, to find out if they could discover the prescription for peace and security in a world constantly at war. Ours is an age of anxiety, but not more so than the centuries between the fall of Constantinople and the Declaration of Independence. Changing appraisals of human nature as well as attitudes toward divine providence produced new preoccupations. Turbulence and expansion stimulated aspirations for improvement.

Americans by 1776 were prepared for republicanism. They had the opportunity of a new country, they had had experience in running their affairs. They had the English political heritage to quote even in criticism of the much admired mixed polity of England about which Tom Paine's *Common Sense* (1776) had done so much to disillusion them. Many of them were well read not only in modern but in ancient history. Human experience, they believed, would teach them much about their own difficult and novel situation. Debates in the critical years reveal both interest in and knowledge of European politics. Eventually a constitution neither purely federative nor fully national and consolidated was created; the document has shown much of the stability hoped for as well as a capacity for survival which could not perhaps have been foreseen, and this in spite of the fact that although the lessons of history were observed they were not always followed. The "one state, one vote" of the United Provinces was instanced as often to show its evils as to show its benefits but in the end was adopted.

How many of the revolutionary generation had read Machiavelli's *Discourses* is uncertain, but both English republicans and Montesquieu had learned from the Italian's work about the conditions under which a republic might be successful. In decline, renewal must be effected. Sometimes a shock like the Roman disaster at Cannae might bring men to a proper sense of their duty. Republics should make use of their wise men in peace as in war. Luxury should be avoided. The laws of change inherent in human nature must be accepted. Statesmen must be continually alert. In republics the general good must be the constant care of the magistrates. They must thus be virtuous, that is, public spirited and courageous. Renewal, a return to first principles—as perhaps now to those of 1776—as well as valor and virtue may save a republic even in its darkest days. Recollection of a noble past may well inspire a better future.[57]

Notes

[1] Charles Francis Adams, ed., *The Works of John Adams*, vol. 4 (Boston, Little and Brown, 1851), p. 15.

[2] *The Dutch Declaration of Independence in 1581*, tr. Lord Somers, Old South Leaflets, vol. 3, no. 72 (Boston, Directors of the Old South Work, 1896).

[3] John Adams, *Diary and Autobiography*, ed. Lyman H. Butterfield, vol. 2 (Cambridge, Belknap Press of Harvard University Press, 1961), p. 240 (hereafter cited as Adams, *Diary*).

[4] Caroline Robbins, "Algernon Sidney's *Discourses Concerning Government*: Textbook of Revolution," *William and Mary Quarterly*, 3d ser., 4(July 1947):267–296.

[5] Élie Halévy, *England in 1815*, 2d ed., tr. E. I. Watkin and D. A. Barker (London, Ernest Benn Limited, 1949), p. 130–139 and references.

[6] *The Works of Tacitus* [translated by T. Gordon] ...*to Which are Prefixed Political Discourses Upon That Author* [by T. Gordon] (London, T. Woodward and J. Peale, 1728-31), vol. 1, "Discourse 5," p. 53. See also Julian Boyd, ed., *The Papers of Thomas Jefferson*, vol. 1 (Princeton, Princeton University Press, 1950), p. 494.

[7] *Encylopédie*, vol. 28 (Amsterdam, 1780), part 2, p. 381.

[8] Andrew Fletcher, "An Account of a Conversation," in his *Works* (Edinburgh, James Bettenham, 1737), p. 365–449, passim. For Franklin and Witherspoon on the Scottish Union, see Adams, *Diary*, vol. 2, p. 248; cf. Max Farrand, ed., *The Records of the Federal Convention of 1787*, rev. ed., vol. 1 (New Haven, Yale University Press, 1966), p. 198, 493 (hereafter *Records*).

[9] David Hume, "The Idea of a Perfect Commonwealth," in his *Political Discourses* (Edinburgh, R. Fleming, 1752), and Montesquieu, *The Spirit of Laws*, vol. 1 (New York, Hafner, 1949), p. 126–128.

[10] Jean Jacques Burlamaqui, *The Principles of Politic Law*, tr. [Thomas] Nugent (London, Printed for J. Nourse, 1752), p. 81–82.

[11] Immanuel Kant, *Perpetual Peace*, tr. M. Campbell Smith (London, Geo. Allen & Unwin, Ltd., 1917), p. 128–137.

[12] Jean Jacques Rousseau, "Considérations sur le gouvernement de Pologne" (ca. 1771), in *The Political Writing of Jean Jacques Rousseau*, ed. Charles E. Vaughan, vol. 2 (Cambridge, Eng., University Press, 1915), p. 442–443. Vaughan translates the sentence about federation on p. 385. See also *Records*, vol. 1, p. 71, 74, 485.

[13] Hezekiah Niles, *Principles and Acts of the Revolution in America* (Baltimore, W. O. Niles, 1822), p. 64–72.

[14] Montesquieu, *The Spirit of Laws*, vol. 1, p. 8.

[15] Jean Bodin, *Six Books of the Commonwealth*, abr. and tr. M. J. Tooley (Oxford, B. Blackwell, 1955), p. 190–193.

[16] Burlamaqui, *Principles*, p. 91–92.

[17] Kant, *Perpetual Peace*, p. 124–125.

[18] Adams, *Works*, vol. 4, p. 303–378.

[19] James Madison, "The Thirty-ninth Federalist." Also see Douglass Adair's article "Experience Must Be Our Only Guide," in *The Reinterpretation of the American Revolution: 1763–1789*, ed. Jack P. Greene (New York, Harper and Row, 1968), p. 397–416.

[20] *Records*, index passim; also note speech by Alexander Hamilton, June 18, 1787, vol. 1, p. 283–293.

[21] George M. Dutcher, "The Rise of Republican Government in the United States," *Political Science Quarterly*, 55(June 1940):199–216. H. A. L. Fisher, in *The Republican Tradition in Europe* (London, Methuen, 1911), virtually ignores republicanism between the Renaissance and the French Revolution.

[22] Adair, "Experience," passim.

[23] *Records*, vol. 1, p. 437; for Price and Montesquieu see the index.

[24] Niles, *Principles,* p. 32, oration at Boston, Mar. 5, 1778.

[25] Adams, *Diary*, vol. 2, p. 247–248, and the Jefferson *Papers*, vol. 1, p. 324–326.

[26] Books providing excellent material on the United Provinces are: Sir William Temple, *Observations Upon the United Provinces of the Netherlands* (London, A. Maxwell for E. Gellibrand, 1673); F. M. Janiçon, *État présent de la République des Provinces-Unies*, 2 vols. (La Haye, 1729); and Guillaume Thomas Raynal, *Histoire du Stadhouderat*, 4th ed. (La Haye, 1748).

[27] *Records*, vol. 1, p. 553.

[28] 1 Samuel 8:11. See also Moses Lowman, *On the Civil Government of the Hebrews* (London, J. Noon, 1740), and James Burgh, *Political Disquisitions*, vol. 1 (London, E. and C. Dilly, 1774), p. 8.

[29] Pieter de la Court, *The True Interest and Political Maxims of the Republick of Holland and West-Friesland,* "written by John de Witt and other great men in Holland" (London, Published by the authority of the States, 1702), p. 369 and passim.

[30] Benedictus de Spinoza, "A Political Treatise," in *Chief Works*, vol. 1 (New York, Dover, 1951), p. 279–387, esp. p. 385 (right to vote) and p. 376 (overthrow of the republic). Perhaps "useless debates" recalls the English Rump and Barebones Parliaments.

[31] William Coxe, *Sketches of the Natural, Civil, and Political State of Swisserland* (Dublin, George Bonham, 1779), letter no. 32, p. 338–350; Algernon Sidney, *Discourses Concerning Government*, vol. 1 (Philadelphia, Printed and published by C. P. Wayne for the Rev. M. L. Weems, 1805), p. 291–292; Montesquieu, *Considerations on the Causes of the Greatness of the Romans and Their Decline*, tr. David Lowenthal (New York, Free Press, 1965), p. 94; Madison, "The Nineteenth Federalist," describing both the German and Swiss confederacies; *Records*, vol. 1, p. 285–286; and Adams, *Works*, vol. 4, p. 313–324, 328–342.

[32] *Records:* vol. 1, p. 112 (Mason) and p. 343 (Wilson), vol. 3, p. 115 (Pinckney). On the equality of the Cantons, see *Records,* vol. 1, p. 454 (Luther Martin), and Adams, *Diary,* vol. 2, p. 204.

[33] Sir Francis d'Ivernois, *An Historical and Political View of the Constitution and Revolutions of Geneva, in the Eighteenth Century* (Dublin, W. Wilson, 1784); Peter Gay, *Voltaire's Politics* (Princeton, Princeton University Press, 1959), p. 185–238; F. M. Arouet de Voltaire, "Idées républicaines," in *Oeuvres completes de Voltaire,* ed. Louis Moland, nouv. ed., vol. 24 (Paris, Garnier frères, 1879), p. 413–432; Adams, *Works,* vol. 4, p. 343–345.

[34] Johann Stephan Pütter, *An Historical Development of the Present Political Constitution of the Germanic Empire,* tr. Josiah Dornford, 3 vol. (London, T. Payne and Son, 1790); *Records,* vol. 4, p. 36; Madison, "The Nineteenth Federalist"; and the Jefferson *Papers,* vol. 1, p. 327.

[35] For example, Samuel Pufendorf, *Of the Law of Nature and Nations* (Oxford, Printed by L. Lichfield, for A. and J. Churchill, 1703), extensively used by John Wise, among others.

[36] A source of much commentary on Italy and Venice is Joseph Addison, *Remarks on Several Parts of Italy...* (London, J. Tonson, 1705). Also useful on Italian republics are: Abraham Nicolas Amelot de La Houssaye, *The History of the Government of Venice* (London, John Starkey, 1677); Jean Gailhard, *The Present State of the Princes and Republicks of Italy* (London, 1668); and Pelatiah Webster, *The Political Union of the United States,* Old South Leaflets, general series, vol. 8, no. 186 (Boston, Directors of the Old South Work, 1907), originally published in Philadelphia, 1783.

[37] James C. Davis, *The Decline of the Venetian Nobility as a Ruling Class* (Baltimore, Johns Hopkins Press, 1962), p. 21–25, is a very clear account of the Venetian system. See also Adams, *Works,* vol. 4, p. 347–357, and *Records,* vol. 1, p. 307, and vol. 2, p. 102. On Maffei see Luigi Rossi, *Un precursore di Montesquieu: Scipione Maffei* (Milano, A. Giuffrè, 1941).

[38] For a brilliant account of the period and excellent remarks on Genoa, see Franco Venturi, *Utopia and Reform in the Enlightenment* (Cambridge, Eng., University Press, 1971).

[39] Adams, *Works,* vol. 4, p. 310–313 (Biscay), p. 303–310 (San Marino). For further material on San Marino, see Niles, *Principles,* p. 78, and *Records,* vol. 1, p. 380.

[40] Franco Venturi, *Saggi sull'Europa Illuminista,* vol. 1, *Alberto Radicati di Passerano* (Turin, G. Einaudi, 1954). Radicati's address to "all lovers of truth and liberty" is included in *Twelve Discourses Concerning Religion and Government* (London, 1734).

[41] Cesare Beccaria, *On Crimes and Punishments,* tr. Henry Paolucci (Indianapolis, Bobbs-Merrill, 1963), p. 8. Beccaria was often quoted in America: Niles, *Principles,* p. 45 (Mason), p. 54 (Minot), p. 100 (Drayton), etc.

[42] M. E. Totze, *The Present State of Europe,* tr. Thomas Nugent, vol. 3, (London, J. Nourse, 1770), p. 107–207 (Sweden); Niles, *Principles,* p. 38 (Tudor); and *Records,* vol. 1, p. 289.

[43] Totze, *The Present State,* vol. 3, p. 209–322; William Coxe, *Travels into Poland, Russia, Sweden, and Denmark,* 3d ed., 4 vols. (London, T. Cadell, 1787), passim;

Adams, *Works*, vol. 4, p. 360–373; and *Records*, vol. 1, p. 290, 459, vol. 2, p. 30, 31, 109–110, and vol. 3, p. 41, 390, 394.

44 Jean Louis de Lolme, *The Constitution of England*, 3d Eng. ed. (London, G. Robinson and J. Murray, 1781); Montesquieu, *Spirit of Laws*, vol. 1, xi, section 6; and Adams, *Works*, vol. 4, p. 358–360.

45 A. S. P. Woodhouse, *Puritanism and Liberty* (London, J. M. Dent & Sons, 1938), and Don M. Wolfe, ed., *Leveller Manifestoes of the Puritan Revolution* (New York, London, Thomas Nelson and Sons, 1944) both print Agreements of the People, as does Old South Leaflets, no. 26.

46 Woodhouse, *Puritanism and Liberty*, p. 66–67.

47 Henry N. Brailsford, *The Levellers and the English Revolution*, ed. Christopher Hill (Stanford, Calif., Stanford University Press, 1961) and Joseph Frank, *The Levellers; a History of the Writings of Three Seventeenth-Century Social Democrats: John Lilburne, Richard Overton, William Walwyn* (Cambridge, Harvard University Press, 1955).

48 Brailsford, *The Levellers*, p. 671–691.

49 Merrill Jensen, *The Founding of a Nation; a History of the American Revolution, 1763–1776* (New York, Oxford University Press, 1968), p. 675; Philip Davidson, *Propaganda and the American Revolution, 1763–1783* (Chapel Hill, N.C., University of North Carolina Press, 1941), p. 33; and Adams, *Diary*, vol. 2, p. 107.

50 Clinton Rossiter, *Seedtime of the Republic; the Origin of the American Tradition of Political Liberty* (New York, Harcourt, Brace, 1953), p. 357. Christopher Hill, in "Republicanism After the Restoration," *New Left Review*, no. 3 (May/June 1960): 46–51, claims that there was some influence but produces no documentation.

51 Marchamont Nedham, *The Excellencie of a Free State* (London, A. Millar and T. Cadell, 1767), p. 2, 33, 38, 47–48. The book was originally published in 1656.

52 Henry Neville, "Plato Redivivus," in Caroline Robbins, ed., *Two English Republican Tracts* (London, Cambridge University Press, 1969), p. 185–188, and Walter Moyle, *The Whole Works* (London, J. Knapton, 1727), p. 62.

53 William B. Gwyn, *The Meaning of the Separation of Powers* (New Orleans, Tulane University, 1965) is an excellent study and includes Nedham's views on separation, p. 131–133.

54 René-Louis de Voyer, Marquis d'Argenson, *Considérations sur le gouvernement ancien et présent de la France* (Amsterdam [i.e. Paris] Marc-Michel Rey, 1765). Chapter 2 surveys other governments and chapter 7 includes d'Argenson's proposed plan, p. 135–199.

55 Montesquieu, *Spirit of Laws*, vol. 1, p. 120, 127–128, and vols. 8 and 9, passim; *The Persian Letters*, ed. J. Robert Loy (New York, Meridian Books, 1961), p. 162, 190, 235, 244; and *Considerations*, passim.

56 *Records*, vol. 3, p. 197 and index. Robert Shackleton, *Montesquieu; a Critical Biography* (London, Oxford University Press, 1961) is the best study.

57 Niccolò Machiavelli, *The Prince and The Discourses* (New York, The Modern Library, 1940), passim and, for "renewal," see p. 397, 538–539; compare Montesquieu's *Considerations*, p. 87–88.

In 1939 J. H. Plumb was elected Ehrman Research Fellow at King's College, Cambridge. Becoming a fellow of Christ's College in 1946, a position which he continues to hold, he was appointed a tutor in 1950 and vice-master in 1964. A lecturer in history at the University of Cambridge from 1946 to 1962, when he was appointed a reader in modern English history, Mr. Plumb was named professor of modern English history in 1966 and was chairman of the history faculty from 1966 to 1968.

Mr. Plumb has served as visiting professor and lecturer at several universities, among them Columbia University in 1960, as Ford's Lecturer at Oxford University in 1966, and as Distinguished Visiting Professor at the City University of New York in 1971. A contributor of articles to professional journals, a book review editor, and a historical advisor to several publishing houses, Mr. Plumb is also an editor of a series of books on European history. Among his published works are England in the Eighteenth Century *(1950, 1968);* Sir Robert Walpole *(1956, 1960);* The First Four Georges *(1956, 1966);* Men and Places *(1963);* Crisis in the Humanities *(1964);* The Growth of Political Stability in England, 1675–1725 *(1967),* American edition; *The Origins of Political Stability in England *(1967);* The Death of the Past *(1970); and* In the Light of History *(1972).*

No SCHOLAR in our own time has illuminated as many facets of England in the 18th century as our next commentator. Whether Walpole, Chatham, the four Georges, or so many other aspects of 18th-century England's political and social climate, J. H. Plumb has brought to it ripe scholarship, wit, insight, and style.

The Fascination of Republican Virtue Amongst the Known and the Unknown

J. H. PLUMB

MISS ROBBINS' PAPER has richly illustrated for us both the complexity of existing republics in Europe before the American Revolution and the varied response—particularly amongst European intellectuals—to that diversity. As she has shown, the best republics possessed that combination which Benjamin Franklin was to symbolize so enduringly for the American people—the prospect of modest riches combined with the practice of steady virtue. As she has told us time and time again in this brilliant excursus of republics and republicans, writer after writer praised republics, partly because, like Venice or Holland, they were rich: somehow economic growth and a republican constitution were indissolubly linked. And partly because republics were not only more tolerant—for even Venice was by Vatican standards almost intolerably tolerant—but also because they were nearer to the needs of social man. They embodied virtue, or seemed to in the minds of men, particularly by what they were contrasted with either directly or by implication.

I would venture to suggest that the fascination with republics was even more widespread in the 18th century, and particularly 18th-century England, than it might seem from Miss Robbins' paper, which, of course, could scarcely be comprehensive within the allotted time, so what I have to say is in no way a criticism but rather an appendix to her paper. After giving us a grand tour of existing republics, she rightly confined her remarks largely to philosophers such as Spinoza or political philosophers such as Harrington or Machiavelli. However, republics fascinated historians perhaps as deeply. I have insufficient time to range as widely as I would like, but there are two whom I would mention: the greatest historian of the age, Edward Gibbon, and perhaps one of the most original English historians of his time, Archdeacon Coxe. Indeed, Archdeacon Coxe does repose in a footnote of Miss Robbins' paper—she uses him to illustrate the fascination with Poland. Poland might interest Archdeacon Coxe, but Switzerland bewitched him. As the tutor to young Lord Herbert, he had travelled there in 1776, a time, after all, when republican ideas were becoming of vivid and immediate importance to Englishmen, and naturally it was not the mountains that brought Coxe and his young charge to Switzerland—*their* appreciation still lay in the future. They studied the constitutions of the Cantons; they watched through roseate spectacles the peasants of the forest cantons striding like old Cato from their farms to undertake their civic duties, and Coxe's prose, usually as unadorned as a steppe, burst into almost lyrical fervor as he described these rustic embodiments of republican virtue. "I really could not have imagined," he wrote to Lady Pembroke on August 5, 1776, "that so almost perfect an equality could have subsisted in any Government. Every Burgher at the age of sixteen has a vote in the General Assembly, which meets annually in an open plain in order to elect new Magistrates, or confirm the old ones, make alliances, war or peace. . . . As to the ill effects of a Democratical Constitution, they are not so common in these little Democracies, where no citizen is rich enough to bribe his fellow citizens to sacrifice their liberty and their happiness as was the case among the Romans." There was, he feels, no corruption in a society whose power and authority lies in the hands of such men as these. When Coxe later published his *Travels in Switzerland*, it acquired almost immediate success—Coxe was writing what a great deal of the British literate public believed to be true, that the best guardian of liberty was the small landowner, for surely the bulwark of British liberties had been its freeholders: a bulwark now sadly breached by the fountains of corruption, graft, and undue aristocratic influence. An idealization of republican virtues was indeed linked with a sense that somehow English political life had been contaminated, a sentiment to which I will return a little later.

But Coxe, of course, was not alone in being fascinated by Switzerland. It attracted a far greater historian—Edward Gibbon—who not only lived there, as we all know, but also very nearly devoted his genius to writing its history. He turned against the idea, he tells us in his *Autobiography*, because it would have meant spending long years reading in a language which he felt to be barbarous—German. Nevertheless, Switzerland did present a real problem for the historian—how could such diverse communities that differed so widely in religion, language, and economic development and that in places were separated by such formidable geographical barriers sustain independence and maintain political stability? Surely here was—and is—a problem worthy of the greatest historical talents. But the real reason, I think, that in the end Switzerland failed to attract Gibbon was its very success: the resonance with his own country was not strong enough. Another idea with which he toyed—Florence of the Medicis—drew him nearer to one of the unconscious springs of his inspiration. Florence presented a drift away from republican virtue into oligarchy and despotism and so echoed his final choice—the mightiest collapse of all of republican virtue—the spread of corruption, graft, violence, and decay in the fall of Rome. These subjects—Florence and Rome—were particularly fascinating, of course, to an Englishman. Remember the year in which Gibbon published his first volume—1776.

Men rarely write history without being deeply influenced by the society in which they are bred and from which they draw their experience of life. And the formative years of Gibbon were an age of increasing sense of frustration, of despair, of a growing belief that somewhere, somehow, England had been betrayed, that the political liberties so dearly won and so rightly established by the Glorious Revolution in 1688 had been violated, that the freeholder had lost and was losing his rights, that political virtue, a sense of citizenship and fraternal belonging, had vanished. Gibbon's exposure of the decay of Rome, the corruption of the old republican virtures, the self-indulgent oligarchy bent on self-gratification, conveyed by analogy a certain genuine bitterness about the England of his time. The sense that somehow Britain had lost its political virtues, that *its* "old Cato," the freeholder, had been betrayed by corrupt aristocratic factions, was quite widespread not only on this side of the Atlantic but also in Britain itself. And there are, if one listens, echoes of this sentiment in Gibbon's majestic prose. But republican sentiment was not the prerogative of the distinguished. It flourished amongst the obscure.

In her seminal book *The Eighteenth Century Commonwealthman*, Miss Robbins has drawn our attention to the leaders of republican sentiment in the fifties and sixties—Thomas Hollis, Catherine Macaulay, Caleb Fleming, and the rest—but one of their casual acquaintances, Sylas Neville, gives us through his diary some sense of the depth as well as the widespread nature of both discontent and of republican sentiment in England itself. Here are a few of his sentiments culled from 1767:

No person is a true friend of liberty that is not a Republican.

The evils of which monarchy is productive should deter any wise nation from submitting to that accursed government.

The Gazette says 10,000 people a year go from the North of Ireland to America and 40,000 in all. May they flourish and set up in due time a glorious free government in that country which may serve as a retreat to those Free men who may survive the final ruin of liberty in this country; an event which I am afraid is at no great distance.

Of course, one might dismiss Neville, as some have, as a disgruntled, illegitimate, aristocratic misfit, but I believe it to be unwise to do so, for he is one of the few sources we have of the widespread nature of frustration amongst ordinary people, of their sense of being victims of corrupt government and that their hope lay, if anywhere, in America. Here are just a sample of the chance conversations that Neville overheard as he wandered through the streets of London. Viewing the Raphael cartoons at Hampton Court, Neville heard a man tell his wife that they would soon belong to the people of England, and at Terry's Coffee House in August 1767 he got into conversation with a stranger who said that he "wished N. America may become free and independent, that it may be an asylum to those Englishmen who have spirit and virtue enough to leave their country, when it submits to domestic or foreign tyranny." And so, one might quote on. Disenchantment with government was very widespread.

I find it hard to believe that Neville's experience was singular and untypical or that the sympathetic sentiments which he seems to have encountered so often were at all unexceptional. After all, when he moved from London to one of the most brutish and least enlightened parts of Norfolk—Scratsby near Great Yarmouth—he found little difficulty in finding kindred spirits to dine with him on calf's head on January 30 in honor of the execution of Charles I, or to share this treasonable toast: "May the example of this day be followed on all like occasions." Surely a powerful republican sentiment!

From the 1760's through the 1780's there was, I believe, a growing sense of the loss of political virtue, that increasingly Englishmen as well as Frenchmen and Americans felt that they were victims of corruption, graft, privilege, and aristocratic exploitation. Whether such was the case is irrelevant—the feeling was intense that governments had lost their virtue. As soon as the Parisian masses erupted in republican fury during the Terror, they at once demanded the creation of primary schools which would teach ethics and the republican virtues. Somehow the 18th-century political nation had got lost; men of all classes, but particularly those who belonged to the *menu peuple*, felt that they had been cheated of their rights, that they were victims of a corrupt machine. It is not surprising that the idealized picture of a republic should appeal to them—honest, free, equal peasants fraternizing in social harmony, taking on their public duties and discharging them virtuously. Hence the idealization in England of the freeholder, in America of the farmer. But the spread of republicanism in the 1760's, along with renewed interest in republics, is due, I think, to that deepening sense of loss, that politics no longer expressed aspiration and could not sustain, let alone extend, liberty.

When such a feeling becomes extensive in the literate public, not only governments but societies themselves become at risk. There are many resonances between our own age and the 18th century, and not least, I think, is the growing sense of despair with government, a deepening criticism that it does not embody equality, fraternity, or liberty—those republican virtues upon which so many hopes were pinned not only in France but here also.

This, however, is to stray far, too far, from Miss Robbins' paper, which has given us new insights into a subject which she has made her own. As long as historians discuss 18th-century republicanism, they will discuss Miss Robbins.

Richard L. Bushman began his teaching career in 1957 as a tutor in American history and literature at Harvard University, from which he took his B.A., M.A., and Ph.D. degrees. After a year in England on a Sheldon Traveling Fellowship, he joined the faculty of Brigham Young University as an assistant professor in 1960. As an interdisciplinary fellow in history and psychology, he taught at Brown University from 1963 to 1965 and at the Wesleyan University summer school, also in 1965. He returned to Brigham Young in the fall and became an associate professor the following year. At the same time he was associate director of the university's honors program and book review editor of Dialogue: A Journal of Mormon Thought. *Professor Bushman was a Fellow of the Charles Warren Center in 1968–69 and then joined the faculty of Boston University, where he has taught for three years.*

Professor Bushman has written numerous articles on religious history and political ideology in 18th-century America. He is the author of From Puritan to Yankee: Character and the Social Order in Connecticut, 1690–1765 *(1967), for which he received the Bancroft Prize, and Editor of* The Great Awakening, Documents on the Revival of Religion, 1740–1745 *(1970).*

SPEAKING AT THE CONSTITUTIONAL CONVENTION, Gouverneur Morris made clear his suspicions of westerners and his belief that "back members are always averse to the best measures." His remarks provoked James Madison to rebuke him for trying to "determine the human character by the points of the compass." Madison reminded Morris of the "truth . . . that all men having power ought to be distrusted to a certain degree." That power corrupts was central to the thinking of the Founding Fathers and to the kinds of safeguards they built into the constitutional system. They had indeed learned their lessons at the hands of masters, the colonial administrators.

This problem of power and corruption is the theme of the paper by Richard Bushman, a profound student of character, religion, and the social order in colonial New England.

Corruption and Power
in Provincial America

RICHARD L. BUSHMAN

CORRUPTION WAS ONE of those heavily encumbered words, so richly and powerfully evocative that it could bear almost limitless usage in 18th-century political discourse. Radical publicists wreathed it in long chains of cognates or partial cognates: luxury, vice, ambition, lust, effeminacy, profligacy. They further defined it by its opposites: virtue, honor, reason, simplicity, benevolence, public spirit, patriotism. It was a word that reached far beyond the confines of politics narrowly conceived to encompass a personal as well as a public morality and to discredit one living style and advance another. But then after sweeping so widely, corruption was always brought to bear finally on public affairs. The ultimate focus of the morality defined by corruption and virtue was politics and the common life. And here all the complex, diffuse meanings boiled down to a simple one: the corrupt indulged their own desires at the expense of the public good, the virtuous put principle and country first. One was selfish, self-indulgent, the other unselfish, disciplined, generous. The degenerate, wrote an American on the eve of the Revolution, "prefer their own mean lucre, the bribes, and the smiles of corruption and arbitrary ministers, to patriotism, to glory, and to the public weal."[1]

In one of its variants, corruption had a still more precise and limited meaning derived from political technology, the ways in which politicians obtained and managed power. It was the meaning one observer had in mind when he said Sir Robert Walpole had "reduced corruption into a regular system." Walpole had brought to perfection the devices for manipulating Parliament which English monarchs had employed for over a century. Either by pressuring voters to choose pliant representatives or by corrupting elected members with pensions, bribes, and offices, the ministry mustered majorities in the Commons to carry government measures. Corruption in this sense was an extension of influence, the illicit form of an acceptable process. Corruption as illicit influence and corruption as selfishness and lust were related as means and ends. The ministry's grip on Parliament allowed men in office to evade the limits which the formal Constitution placed on power, thus giving license to their wanton ambition. And it was greed and lust for power which drove the ministry's devious campaign to subvert the Commons. The base desire and the method for realizing it were so closely related that calling both corruption confused no one.[2]

Corruption as influence lay at the very heart of English political processes in the 18th century. Politics cannot be reduced solely to the manipulation of places, pensions, and connections, as was once thought, but the instruments of corruption were the machinery of parliamentary management and, more important, corruption was the notion by which important segments of the political community understood and explained politics to themselves and their constituents. The opposition in the Commons, radical publicists commenting from the sidelines, and many of the country members perceived one form of corruption or another working against bills that they favored and holding in power ministers whom they despised. Corruption explained the failure of good men and patriotic measures. It was a master category for comprehending politics and, in fact, led ultimately toward parliamentary reform in the succeeding century.

Was corruption a master category in the colonies too? Did provincial Americans understand their political processes in the same way? The question is important for understanding the origins of the Revolution, for we know that corruption was a key idea for the radicals who led the colonists toward independence. Not that in sheer bulk the corruption of the legislature looms very large in revolutionary literature. In the public appeals it was introduced briefly, sometimes apparently tangentially. And yet it was a critical hinge in the argument, for it explained events that otherwise were confusing. It explained why the Constitution had failed to contain rulers and shed light on their hidden motives. It made the sequence of events after 1764 appear to be not a series of regrettable mistakes but a design, a "history of repeated injuries and usurpations all having in direct object the establishment of an absolute tyranny." It is an idea whose genealogy we must trace in our quest for the origins of a revolutionary temperament.

We know that by the 1750's, well before the imperial crisis, there were outspoken colonists who had assimilated the opposition vision of politics. In virtually all of the political centers in America, men of influence and standing, not mere ephemeral agitators, were in touch with one element or another of the English opposition and were broadcasting through the American press conceptions of government taken directly from *Cato's Letters*, *The Craftsman*, *The Independent Whig*, and the tendentious histories of Denmark, Rome, and Germany. Although it is difficult to estimate just how widely held radical doctrines were in the 1750's, at the very least a firm beachhead had been established. Radical ideas had a base from which they could spread as events confirmed their dire predictions about the demise of English liberty.[3]

The still puzzling question is how characteristic and endemic were opposition ideas in the previous half-century. Was the fear of corruption in high places the common belief of colonial politicians? Did it shape their attitudes toward their own governors? Were they as alert to attempts to subvert the legislature and upend the Constitution as their English counterparts? In short, were the radical components of revolutionary political thought mid-century imports or were they by 1750 already well-integrated elements of colonial political culture?

In a larger sense the issue is not merely the genesis of a particular critical idea in revolutionary thought. The question really is how did Americans conceive of their own political processes. Did they see politics as an unending war against legislative corruption, as a constant defense of their liberties against an executive who unscrupulously manipulated patronage to undermine and circumvent the constitutional checks on his power? In other words, did colonials understand politics in the same terms as did commonwealthmen in England? Were American politics, in colonial eyes, a replication on a smaller scale of politics in the mother country? Did the revolutionary ideology of corruption and conspiracy flow naturally and inevitably from the everyday experience of provincial politicians?[4]

Of all the colonies, none is better suited for a study of political ideas than Massachusetts. Its vigorous press, its succession of newspapers, and its published legislative journals disclose the opinions of the political community as fully as in any 18th-century province.[5] If radical notions of political corruption had any currency in the colony, traces should remain in the outpourings of its presses. For the literature issuing from the Massachusetts General Court, the question of corruption is easily answered. On the public surface anyway, in addresses to governor and crown and in reports of house committees, corruption simply does not figure. There were no accusations against the governor, no implications that he manipulated the legislators with patronage or interfered with elections in the towns. The issues which most troubled the assembly from the arrival of the first royal governor in 1692 until the removal of Jonathan Belcher in 1741 are the classic constitutional issues with which we have long been familiar: the right of the house to elect its speaker, the right to audit accounts and control expenditures, the right to adjourn itself, an annual versus a permanent salary for the governor. If we except the equally familiar controversies over currency and the mast forests, the long term issues which most often preoccupied the house were all connected with their privileges as a legislative body and are reminiscent of Parliament's struggles with the crown in the previous century. The intent in every case was to preserve the representatives' right to consent against executive harassment or limitation. The deputies insisted on the untrammeled choice of a speaker so that no dependent of the governor could interfere with their proceedings. They argued for the right to adjourn to escape the pressures of protracted sessions, a tactic Massachusetts governors used more than once. The house refused more than one year's salary to their governors to maintain the balance of power between them and claimed the right to audit accounts as part of the cherished right to tax and appropriate.[6]

However tense and indignant the antagonists became in those ever-recurring contests, the house never gave way to its anger. None of the effusive charges of corruption found in revolutionary literature erupted in the official rhetoric of the Massachusetts legislature. During one fight with Jonathan Belcher, the house impatiently snapped at the governor: "How therefore your Excellency could utter such things of the House, is astonishing." But then the deputies went on to state their fundamental position: "All that this or former Assemblies have endeavoured is, to preserve the

Powers granted by CHARTER to the General Court, in making Laws. . . ."
That is what the contests always came to, a debate over the exact definition
of constitutional rights. The governors and representatives filled their exchanges with close readings of the charter, the citation of precedents, and
references to parallel cases in England, and finally, after exhausting their
stock of arguments, appealed to England for adjudication. In the General
Court the legal framework of formal governmental processes seemed successfully to have contained all the animosity generated in the disputes.[7]

The lower house throughout the controversies seemed determined to
observe the proprieties which 18th-century political theory demanded. It
refused to demean the governor's character or imply malfeasance. Even
while the government was riven with conflict the house never lost sight
of the elusive ideal of harmony and respect for rulers and consciously
avoided censoriousness. At loggerheads with William Burnet over his
salary, the representatives nonetheless assured him that

we have always been careful that our Consultations and Conclusions thereabout, might
be managed in the most decent and respectful manner; chusing to say less than the
Subject would bear, and no more, than what the Nature of the thing and Faithfulness
to the People required; lest by a too close and critical disquisition of this matter, something should drop that might be offensive, and interrupt that Harmony and good
Understanding between Your Excellency and this House, which is so conducive to
Your Ease, so necessary to the publick Good, and so very much desired and valued
by Us. . . .[8]

House documents, as would be expected, are replete with expansive as-
sertions of loyalty to the House of Hanover, to the person of the king, and
to the royal prerogative, but the assembly was also at pains to prove in the
record that nothing they said or did could justly be "accounted disrespect-
ful to your Excellancy" and that "every thinking Man amongst us" confessed that it tended "greatly to their Honour and benefit, at all times to
Pay due Respects to the Kings Governours." All this was written in full
awareness that contrary behavior "when Represented Home, will turn to
their disadvantage." Court conventions required the representatives to
mind their tongues. An implication of disrespect, even of neglect of duty,
much less of corruption, would be seen at once as seditious and bring down
the wrath of the crown. But the point is that the house observed the conventions, scrupulously minded its tongue, and while it did, only the desire
for harmony and regard for the governor appeared in its printed journals
amidst the lengthy arguments over constitutional rights. The assembly itself
never was and could not be the medium for advertising the presence of
corruption among the colony's rulers.[9]

The restraint of official documents does not mean that the whole mind of the popular party in the assembly was equally antiseptic. The house's comment to Burnet in 1728 that they chose "to say less than the Subject would bear" for fear of dropping something "that might be offensive" and interrupt the desired "Harmony and good Understanding" suggests some kind of suppressed animosity working below the surface. The House of Commons similarly couched its opening address to the throne in the most circumspect language and followed it with debate that could become brutally frank. The mind of the opposition in the Commons can fully be known only from unofficial writings. It was in anonymous pamphlets and newspaper essays that opposition members enlarged upon their suspicions of corruption in the ministry and elaborated their characteristic view of politics.[10]

Was there an equivalent to the English opposition press in provincial Massachusetts, one which reveals the true feelings of the popular party? There certainly were publications written against the government or, more generally, against the ruling orders. Some 40 such pamphlets appeared in Massachusetts between 1695 and 1740, besides two noteworthy newspapers with an antiestablishment flavor. Boston newspapers for the most part were innocuous collections of foreign dispatches and bland local news, but James Franklin's *New England Courant*, in its first two years of publication from 1721 to 1723, was a barbed, pungent paper modeled after English opposition journals. Not only did it borrow from English publicists—complete essays as well as excerpts from *Cato's Letters* were reprinted in the *Courant* —but it engaged in sallies of its own against government. *The Weekly Rehearsal*, while under the editorship of the Boston attorney Jeremiah Gridley from 1731 to 1733, was a polite and somewhat pale imitation of the *Courant*. Local authors did not comment on current political issues or indulge themselves as English radicals did in discourses on the evils of power, but the *Weekly Rehearsal* did reprint essays from *The Free Briton*, *Fog's Journal,* and *The London Magazine* which exposed readers to radical ideas.[11]

Taking newspapers and pamphlets together, only a few publications were as vitriolic or forthright as *The Craftsman* or *Cato's Letters* or any number of English essayists, but the corrupt ruler does come on the scene from time to time, manipulating the legislature through patronage and electoral influence. He appears in the person of Governor Dudley in a pamphlet published in London in 1708 and reprinted in Boston in 1720. Dudley, it was said, "so Modelled the General Assembly, that they shall pass wretched Votes to his Advantage, and Kiss the Hand which all the open Eyes in the Country see Stabbing of them." The advice to oppose placemen was offered more or less incidentally in three currency tracts in 1720 and 1721, the most direct in *A Letter to an Eminent Clergyman*:

It is of very Great Importance, what sort of Man you have for Representatives, therefore it highly Concerns your several Towns: to send Good, Honest and Trusty Men: those who have no Commissions, nor any dependence on the Government, are certainly the best men, and so you will find it. Men that will make themselves Tools to a party, or are meerly passive, and will suffer themselves to be led by the Nose, are fit for no publick Trust. . . .

James Franklin, both in the *Courant* and in pamphlets issuing from his press, warned against electing "Sheriffs, Military Officers, and the like," or "indeed, any one that hath a Place of Profit deriving from the Government." So few "are able to withstand the Snares and Temptations that Places of Honour and Profit subject them to. . . ." They "become Wax to receive every Impression the Enemies of our Constitution shall think fit to make on them," mere implements of power, "a Tool and a Property to another," all "for the sake of Preferment."[12]

Beyond any doubt there were writers in Massachusetts, familiar with English ideas of corruption, speaking out against management of the assembly. And there must have been an audience of believers, at the very least a group of tavern radicals in Boston. But were they spokesmen for the popular party? Did the radical pamphleteers represent the opinion of the governor's opposition in the assembly in the way that the *Craftsman* spoke for Walpole's enemies in the Commons? Did James Franklin reveal the mind of Elisha Cooke, the leader of the popular party, and the large body of representatives who relied on Cooke to argue for popular rights against the prerogative? In short, was the fear of corruption, the real heart of provincial politics, the driving force behind the formal debates over charter privileges?

I doubt very much that Cooke or the popular party in the assembly inspired the *Courant* as Pulteney and Bolingbroke inspired the *Craftsman*, if only because Franklin and the assembly obviously were not pulling together. The *Courant* appeared in the midst of a crisis that ultimately sent Governor Shute flying to England. The assembly refused to yield on a long list of claims which the governor believed invaded the royal prerogative: the annual salary, the right to adjourn, disposition of troops, auditing of accounts, proprietorship of the mast trees, and the election of a speaker. At the very time when controversy came to a peak in the assembly, the *Courant* was in full flower, and yet it scarcely touched on any of those issues. There were glancing references to the audit of accounts and to the mast tree dispute, but on the vital questions of the speaker and adjournment, not a word. The *Courant* began publication with a series of attacks on inoculation, with Cotton Mather as target, and later took swings at the whole clerical establishment. So strong is this animus in the *Courant's* pages that Perry Miller discussed the paper in a chapter called "Antiministerial Sentiment." From all this the assembly was isolated. Criticism of the clergy simply was not on its agenda, nor was the house tolerant of such abuse. In 1722 Franklin printed a pamphlet commending the assembly for earlier refusing a bill to prevent "factious and scandalous Papers," but that modicum of sentiment for a free press was not enough to protect the *Courant.* Less than a year after Franklin's first issue, the house and council imprisoned him for "a High affront to this Government," and when that did not inhibit his criticisms, the court took more drastic action. The committee report adopted by both houses found the printer guilty of contempt for religion, abuse of the Scriptures, injurious reflections on ministers, and insults to His Majesty's government. He was forbidden to publish without first submitting copy to the province secretary, a return to licensing procedures abandoned in England long before. The assembly that gagged Franklin was not a docile House of Commons either. It was in these years that the popular party was tallying near-unanimous votes against the prerogative. And yet there was nothing precious enough in the *Courant* to give the house a moment's pause before striking the paper down.[13]

The *New England Courant* was not the outlet for the repressed feelings of the popular party. James Franklin is better seen as a printer and journalist than a party hack. He hoped to sell newspapers by publishing a daring imitation of the radical London journals and was probably less committed to his ideas than to his business. He is important less for his following than for his function as an importer of radical English whiggery. Not only did he reprint the latest sensation of the London press, *Cato's Letters,* but he evoked native writing in the same slashing style. He in effect instructed Massachusetts in current English political fashions well before political leaders were prepared to adopt them. Quite appropriately Franklin called his tract touching on electoral corruption *English Advice to the Freeholders, etc. of the Province of Massachusetts Bay.*

Entrenched as it was in the assembly, the popular party felt no need for an opposition press in 1722, nor for many years thereafter. The published journals of the house, given to every member for distribution in his town, served perfectly well so long as the opposition wrote the addresses and the reports directed against the governor. The controversies continued in full vigor up to Belcher's removal in 1741, and no journal appeared to take the

Courant's place. *The Weekly Rehearsal* printed lively essays on modish themes, but its deepest excursion into radical politics was republication of general essays from London papers. *The Weekly News-Letter, The Boston Gazette* started in 1719, the post-1723 *Courant, The New England Weekly Journal*, first issued in 1727, and *The Boston Weekly Post-Boy* begun in 1734 were all perfectly circumspect. *The Boston Evening Post*, the successor to *The Weekly Rehearsal* in 1735, later spoke out against the government, but not before 1740. From 1695 to 1740 there were only two years in which a radical newspaper was sold in Boston. Political comment in the weeklies was limited to official reports and speeches and petitions and addresses to the throne and governor. If political opinion were formed by the sheer volume of input, the decorous rhetoric of the assemblies and the royalist language of officials and king would be far and away the most powerful influences on the province. Pamphlets were similarly restrained. For a decade and a half after 1722 no tracts matched those of the previous two years in their bluntness. Seemingly none of the colony's politicians provided incentives for printers to offer forthright political comment on corruption. In 1739, when an anonymous pamphleteer calling himself "Americanus" wrote again in the spirit of Franklin, quoted Cato, and renewed warnings of the pernicious influence of patronage, no one in Boston would print his tract. By his own confession he had to send to Rhode Island to have it published.[14]

If there existed a fear of corruption in the characteristic mode of the English opposition, it rarely appeared in print in Massachusetts. Excluding Franklin's small output, in all the pamphlets written against the ruling orders or in defense of the assembly, there are only six references to corruption of the legislature by the executive. One is from the Americanus who went begging for a publisher, one is an incidental aside in an indictment of Dudley, and three are passing comments in currency tracts in 1720 and 1721. The one pamphlet which enlarges on gubernatorial influence with anything like the relish of a London publicist is *The Deplorable State of New England*, printed in London in 1708 to discredit Dudley. And that tract was written for an English audience, most likely by an English author, and would understandably play upon English stereotypes of corruption, by then a convention of the literature of political derogation. None of the complaints clearly attributable to New Englanders charged him with corrupting the legislature.[15]

In Massachusetts such talk simply could not be made to sound persuasive. The means of exercising influence were so obviously absent. Cato had declared that the only way to "preserve the publick liberty" in a monarchy was by "frequent fresh Elections of the People's Deputies," and that was precisely what Massachusetts had: annual elections. No small bodies of town leaders, susceptible to pressures from local magnates, monopolized the election of representatives as they did in England. Every 40-shilling freeholder, a large proportion of the adult males, could vote. The Massachusetts Assembly was a reformed House of Commons from the outset. Voting was even by ballot. In the *New England Courant*'s most elaborate diatribe against influence, the author was driven to great lengths to explain exactly how, in spite of all, Major Ball-Face, a "Tool and Property" of the administration, could intimidate others. In a town election James Trueman, who was indebted to Ball-Face for a license, failed to vote for one of the Ball-Face clan. The major discovered Trueman in his base act of ingratitude by a mark left on the ballot when he voted with a bloody finger. Only by sheer chance could Ball-Face get at one voter; how much harder to sway an entire town.[16]

After election, representatives who benefited from the governor's largesse in one way or another did take the governor's side more often than others.[17] But patronage certainly did not guarantee control of their votes. Judging from the titles of the representatives in each year's list up to 1740, usually over a third were militia officers or justices of the peace. And yet these same deputies voted in large majorities against the prerogative on constitutional issues. The popular party always controlled the house. Had patronage swayed more deputies, place bills to exclude officeholders from the legislature would have been laid before the assembly. The opposition in Parliament almost ritualistically introduced them in the Commons to blunt the ministry's influence. In Massachusetts during these years the question of the appointment of deputies to offices in the governor's patronage never arose. So far as I can tell, no bill was even introduced. The representatives gratefully accepted their commissions from the governor and then blithely voted against him when they chose, confident of immunity from retribution. No one thought to deprive them of the combined privileges of their elective and appointive positions.[18]

In sum, there is precious little evidence that the legislature was corrupted in the towns where the deputies were chosen or in the capital where patronage was dispensed. The great question which agitated England throughout the 18th century never emerged in Massachusetts before midcentury. In England the exercise and restraint of crown influence lay at the heart of the most crucial constitutional issues, generated a huge political correspondence among magnates and lesser lights, and provided unlimited grist for the radical mill. In Massachusetts there is no political correspondence dealing with places and influence. Constitutional developments turned on other issues, and journalists only infrequently pretended to discover creatures of the governor among the deputies. The lower house, never pliant, on critical constitutional questions almost invariably opposed the governor. Massachusetts may have been close to being the uncorrupted country which colonists who compared it to England thought it to be.[19]

What standing then did the fear of corruption have in the provincial political mind? Are we to conclude that Massachusetts politicians were possessed above all by a scrupulous devotion to constitutional rights, as the legislative documents lead us to believe, with no clear idea of the corruptions of power, no active apprehensions of executive malevolence? We would err, of course, if we underestimated the importance of constitutional rights. The colonists were deeply committed to the protection of their right to consent, not merely out of admiration for Parliament, but because that right sustained their feeling of dignity, security, and freedom. But we would also err if we attributed an innocence to colonial politicians, a trust in power which was not theirs.

Massachusetts politicians were indeed wary of corruption; they doubted the integrity of officials, especially their governors; they frankly voiced these suspicions; and what is more, the fear of corruption underlay many of the popular party's most critical controversies with the governor. But it was corruption of another sort, derived from the general meaning of the word, the selfish indulgence of base desires, a much simpler corruption unrelated to the intricacies of the balanced Constitution. It was nothing more than the ancient fear of rulers' greed, covetousness as the clergy called it, the belief that men in power used their offices to enrich themselves at the expense of the people. They could not ordinarily speak of avarice in the everyday exchanges in the assembly, but in complaints to the crown, in indictments written after a governor's removal, and in anonymous pamphlets the underlying uneasiness comes to light.[20]

In dispute after dispute, these suspicions coursed just below the surface of the conventional respect and trust which the assembly ordinarily took such pains to keep intact. The tracts which followed the overthrow of Andros, when all inhibitions were removed, overflowed with resentment of official avarice. The misery of living under an illegal Constitution was the license it gave the governor and his creatures to enrich themselves. They were able to extort intolerable fees because they were unrestrained by "any Rules but those of their own insatiable Avarice and Beggary." The governor challenged land titles so as to wrest them from the rightful owners and measure them out "for his Creatures." Throughout the administration, New England was "squeez'd by a Crew of abject Persons fetched from *New York*, to be the Tools of the Adversary." "All that we counted dear was made a Prize To th' raging Lust and hungry Avarice Of a few tater'd Rascals from New York."[21]

The taint of Andros' avarice lingered about Joseph Dudley, a Massachusetts native, who had been president of the council before Andros' arrival and who from 1702 to 1715 governed the province himself under royal commission. When he was thought to be implicated in illicit trade with the French, provincial politicians were irate. Both house and council, under duress, cleared the governor, but Cotton Mather, less inhibited than the assembly, bluntly told him

Sir, your snare has been that thing, the hatred whereof is most expressly required of the ruler, namely Covetousness. . . . The main channel of that Covetousness has been the reign of bribery, which you, Sir, have set up in the land, where it was hardly known till you brought it in fashion.

Samuel Sewall, then of the council and under great pressure from Dudley to conform, thought the governor was too tolerant of bribery. In a dramatic encounter in the council chamber, Sewall withdrew his vote to clear Dudley of suspicion. His brother afterwards told him "the generality of thoughtful people" approved his "Mount Etna Eruption," as he called it. In the next election of councilors, Sewall received 98 of 99 possible votes from the representatives, more than any other councilor. Sewall's implicit rebuke of Dudley probably spoke more truly for the feelings of the house than the resolution clearing him of corruption. A memorial sent from New England urging the queen to appoint a new governor said "One principal Grievance, which Comprehends many under it, is, The Course of Bribery, which runs thro' the Governour's Administration. . . ." Another memorial, sold in Boston in 1707, accused the governor and his son Paul of "not being content with what Money they come fairly by, and over greedy for Gain" and of being "very Screwing and Exacting upon the People." "They are so Mercenary, there is no Justice to be had without Money." The furor blew over in time, but Dudley never enjoyed the full confidence of the province. Late in his administration, in an address to the queen, the deputies struck out a phrase saying they were satisfied with Dudley's disposition of the colony's money. He was always suspected of pursuing his "mercenary interest" above the public good.[22]

Similar suspicions pursued every administration. Advocates of a private land bank grounded their argument in large part on the fear that the governor and council would put the bank's money to their own uses. "We have always looked upon it, That an empty Treasury is very much our Security," one tract declared in 1714. A few years later the governor refused to confirm the elected speaker of the house for saying that the surveyor of woods was "daily selling and Bartering" the king's trees "for filthy lucre," "wresting Monies from the poor People to inrich himself." The agents for the house of representatives in 1729 complained of Governor Burnet that he had "made the general good and welfare of the whole Province subservient to his own private particular interest, and hath seemed by his words and actions to have no other end or view in coming to preside over them but to consult his own advantage."[23]

These were not the feverish outpourings of ephemeral journalists or coffeehouse radicals. They represented the sentiments of leaders of the popular party in the house of representatives and usually of the majority of deputies. Elisha Cooke, the most eminent figure in the popular party, backed the private bank in 1714, trying to keep bank funds out of reach of government officials. Cooke also was the one to charge the royal surveyor of woods with schemes to defraud colonists and king of their rights in the Maine forests. It was the house of representatives that instructed its agents to denounce Burnet for putting private interest first. Most important, the house tried in every way it could to pass into law restrictions on the misapplication of funds. On no other issues, except the permanent salary, did they resist the executive more strenuously than on the audit and regulation of public money. Unlike corruption of the legislature, which never called forth legislation, the threat of official avarice was the base for concerted legislative action. Conventional respect for rulers inhibited criticism in official documents, but the deputies' actions showed how they felt.[24]

The assembly's struggle to regulate the management of provincial moneys lasted almost exactly as long as the more notorious salary dispute and caused almost as much furor. The goal from first to last was to prevent withdrawals from the treasury for purposes which the house had not approved. In 1694, while still smarting from memories of Andros' abject crew of New York harpies, the assembly declared that "no publick money be or ought to be disposed of by his excellency the governour, and council, but for the uses and intents" specified in acts "of the entire Court." The Privy Council disallowed the act, but the impulse behind it could not be quenched. Despite Dudley's pointed reassurance of the "Queen's extraordinary Care in the Disposition of her revenue, which all her Servants are Bound to Imitate," the house claimed "the undoubted Privilege of concurring" in "the particular Application and Disposal of all and every Sum and Sums that are put into the Treasury." They wished to protect that privilege by requiring that every warrant from the governor and council indicate from which account in the original appropriation the money was to be withdrawn and by approving the warrants themselves before the treasurer honored them. In effect the house desired an equal part in the executive's traditional right to dispose of public money. The house could see no other way of guaranteeing that tax funds were not misapplied.[25]

In 1721 amidst a house investigation into manipulations of the muster rolls submitted by militia officers with their requests for reimbursements, the representatives achieved the control they had sought since 1694. The council and, for some unexplained reason, the governor approved a tax bill which required that every warrant specify the particular account on which it drew and which gave the house the right to approve each warrant before the treasurer paid out the money. Two years later, when the council belatedly recognized how annoyingly scrupulous the house intended to be, the board protested the loss of executive autonomy and asked for a return to the former method of managing the treasury. By then it was too late to go back. For eight years the house exercised its extraordinary powers with little hindrance, until Governor Burnet in 1729, in the middle of his do-or-die attempt to wring a permanent salary from the assembly, objected to the form of the tax bill as well. Burnet died before the issue was resolved, and Lt. Gov. William Dummer, Burnet's temporary replacement, acquiesced in the house's demand, but by then the issue was in England. In 1730 the 30th instruction to the governor of the province forbade the house to audit accounts before payment. Governor Belcher arrived in that year committed to renewing the controversy Burnet had begun. Unabashed by the pronouncement of the king's will and pleasure, the assembly, now with the council's backing, refused by a vote of 57 to 1 to alter the form of appropriation. "Your Excellency may be as well assured," the house told Belcher,

> that as long as this Assembly retain any regard to the great trust and confidence our Electors have put in us, all efforts to perswade and induce us to forsake their true Interest and bring them and their Posterity under the weight and burden of such innumerable and inconceivable inconveniences as the House firmly believe may soon be their lot and portion, should the House give into the aforesaid Instruction

will fail. "Such a concession would be to act against the light of our own Reason and Conscience." While appealing to both the king and the House of Commons for a withdrawal of the 30th instruction, the house refused for two years to refill the province treasury.[26]

Ultimately the assembly had to give way. The king in council and the Commons turned their plea aside and confirmed the right of the governor and council to make withdrawals. Meanwhile militia officers, justices of the peace, and all the other creditors of the province went without pay. Holding back the governor's salary until he accepted a one-year grant hurt only the governor; waiting on a tax bill affected the deputies' constitutents. In 1733 an acceptable tax bill was submitted. The attorney general permitted the house to appropriate taxes for particular uses, but after 1733 it never again audited accounts before payment. For all their determination, the representatives could not devise a strategy for sustaining their claim.[27]

Neither the suspicion of avarice, which nerved the deputies in their dispute with the governors, nor the resort to legal controls were American innovations. The greed of the ministry troubled the Country Party in England as much as illicit influence in the legislature. The two forms of lust and deviousness merged imperceptibly in England into a single image of corruption. Parliamentary commissions of accounts to inhibit avarice were as much a Country Party reform as the perpetual place bills. Throughout the 18th century, the opposition jealously eyed the treasury and hinted darkly of peculation. Massachusetts could borrow one doubt as easily as the other; the origins of this element of provincial political culture are not hard to locate. What is more perplexing is the balance of their apprehensions. Massachusetts politicians said little about influence and did less. There were no place bills, no legislative efforts of any kind in this half-century to contain that kind of corruption. On the other hand, the fear of avarice was overblown, the efforts to control the treasury excessive. The Commons could not possibly endorse the assembly's insistence on auditing accounts before payment because the Commons itself did not enjoy that privilege. As a committee of the Privy Council reported, "if your Majesty should withdraw Your Instruction on this Head, the Assembly of Massachusetts-Bay would be left in possession of a Power superiour to any which the British House of Commons lay Claim to in Cases of the same Nature." Parliament was permitted exactly what the 30th instruction allowed to Massachusetts: the right to examine accounts annually after payment had been made. Royal officials were understandably scornful of the assembly's presumption.[28]

Why was Massachusetts, by English standards, so obsessed with official avarice, so determined to restrict the governor's use of public money? Apart from Burnet's imposition of a new and illegal fee for clearing vessels, there were no proven cases of financial depredations among Massachusetts governors from William Phips through Jonathan Belcher. Dudley's complicity in the French trade remained a mere suspicion until he died. Only a thin flow of rumor about a Cornbury in New York or a Cranfield in New Hampshire nourished the prevalent apprehensions. Contemporaries judged officials in England to be far more given to their lust for the profits of office. Their venality stunned American visitors, who came home rejoicing in the comparative purity of government in the New World.[29] Why then the extravagant suspicions of their own governors who were comparatively innocent?

The colonists themselves gave an answer. Their qualms had more to do with the governors' incongruous social and political position than with their moral faults. The governors did not meet the conventional expectations for a good ruler's qualifications. As a group most of imported officialdom, in the colonists' eyes, had two damning faults: they were poor and they were strangers. It was commonly assumed that political authority and social eminence were of a piece. Rulers should be distinguished by family, education, and wealth, not simply for the sake of hierarchical symmetry but because eminent men were on the whole thought to be more trustworthy. Thomas Pownall, a later Massachusetts governor, said the colonists would only give their confidence to a "considerable person," for "they would know that there, there was no spirit of party or faction; that there there could be no jobb." The colonial governors held a position in their sphere as important as the lords lieutenants in England, and yet few were of comparable social magnitude. The Massachusetts governors, while not an undistinguished lot, certainly did not measure up to that standard. In the colonists' mind, the archetypal governor was the man of broken fortune or of new wealth, an aspiring and ambitious man, the very sort thought most capable of jobbing and spoliation. They were an easy lot to caricature: "A poor naked hungry Governour comes usually from the Court every three years, with a troop of miserable, debauched Followers ... whose Debaucheries, Ignorance and Necessities, provoke them to innumerable Practices of Fraud and Violence." In his *Defence of the New England Charters,* published in 1721, Jeremiah Dummer, the colony's agent, took it for granted that "the View that Governours generally have is private Gain," and explained why.

It can hardly be expected but that these Corruptions must happen when one considers that few Gentlemen will cross the Seas for a Government, whose Circumstances are not a little streight at Home, and that they know by how slight and uncertain Tenure they hold their Commissions; from whence they wisely conclude, that no Time is to be lost.

Dummer did not have to belabor the point. It was obvious that when indebted and necessitous men took colonial posts, they would indulge their unsatisfied hunger for the profits of office.[30]

More important still, the governors were damned for being alien. Unlike English county officials, who were drawn from prominent local families with roots deep in the communities over which they officiated, the governors were foreign placemen, imposed on the province from without. It was not so much that the governors were not Puritans or that they were habituated to the modes of another culture. The crucial matter was their interests. The private interests of a newly arrived governor did not align him with the interests of the colony. Without property or family in Massachusetts, a Governor Shute or Burnet had no reason not to defraud the colony. Jonathan Belcher, one of the three Massachusetts men to occupy the governor's chair, was valued as "a native of New England, of a good clear paternal estate, and consequently of a true natural interest in the country...." One of Andros' failings was that he "did adhere principally to the advice of a few strangers, who were persons without an interest in the country, but of declared prejudice against it, and had plainly laid their designs to make an unreasonable *profit* of the poor people." Thomas Hutchinson thought it obvious why people allied against the prerogative rather than dividing evenly between monarchical and popular parts of the constitution as they did in England. In the colonies "people, in general, consider the prerogative as an interest, without them, seperated and distinct from the interior interest of the colony...."[31]

Eventually the Massachusetts House explained that the divergence of interests was the reason they dared not grant the governors a permanent salary. When the question of an annual grant versus a fixed salary had first arisen shortly after the institution of the new charter, the assembly had argued in traditional, legalistic terms. It was their undoubted right derived from the charter commission to levy money and appropriate it. In 1728 for the first time a royal governor pressed hard for the salary, and seemed determined to hold the assembly in session until he got it. Then the legalistic overlay began to peel off. Governor Burnet demanded to know why he was refused a salary when the king was granted the civil list for life. Why did Massachusetts insist on restraining the executive even more than Parliament? The assembly acknowledged that they could not possibly confide "in any Governour whatsoever so much as in our most

Gracious King," and then explained why. The king's "Interest and Glory, and that of his Royal Progeny, are inseperable from the prosperity and welfare of his People; Whereas it is most obvious that ordinarily neither the Prosperity nor Adversity of a People affect a Governour's Interest at all, when he has once left them." At this stage in the debate, the deputies sandwiched the comment on the conflict of interest among a variety of constitutional arguments about balancing power. Three months later, after Burnet had moved the house to Salem, the furious representatives petitioned the king. Then all others fell away and "one chief reason" against a fixed salary came forward:

The Governor should be induced by his own interest, as well as duty to your Majesty, to consult the interest and welfare of the people, but should we fix a sallary, the Governor's particular interest would be very little affected (while thus settled) by serving or disserving the people's interest. ... Neither the happiness nor the adversity of this Province, affect a Governor's interest, when he has once left us. ...

Only his dependence on the assembly for a salary gave the governor some inducement to consult the welfare of the province as well as his own. In that moment the assembly's reason for guarding its constitutional privilege so militantly at last came into the open. The colony could not trust a ruler whose private interests did not mingle with its own.[32]

This was how provincial Massachusetts saw its political situation.[33] The house clung to every constitutional right, and especially the right to control public funds, as a safeguard against indigent and alien placemen sent from England to govern. This perception of politics did not mean local men were thought to be exempt from suspicion. Covetousness was a leading temptation for every ruler, a Dudley or a Belcher as well as a Shute or Burnet. But the alien placeman was, of course, much more susceptible, and in the colonists' minds, he was the typical appointee. The assembly could not grant a permanent salary to a favored governor, for it knew full well that concessions granted one year to a trustworthy man could be exploited the next by an avaricious court dependent, the colonists' idea of the characteristic governor.

This judgment of typicality was based on a realistic if pessimistic assessment of America's place in the empire. Simply because political rewards fueled the British political machinery, and because there never were enough places, one of the army of office-seekers in the home country, supplicating the dispensers of patronage, was more likely to be appointed than a native politician with his roots in the colony. And as Dummer said, since few gentlemen "will cross the Seas for a Government, whose Circumstances are not a little streight at Home," the governors were not likely to be men of fortune. It followed from the realities of Anglo-American politics that the typical appointee would not be native, distinguished, or wealthy and therefore would be unusually susceptible to temptation. Deficient rulers were one of the ineluctable consequences of Massachusetts' provincial status.

Massachusetts was not alone in its misgivings about royal officials. It was a commonplace among colonial political observers that governors "have it in their Power to gripe and squeeze the People" all for "their own private Gain." In the last chapter of his book on the colonies, Edmund Burke listed as one of three major problems, the "old complaint, that it is not easy to bring American governors to justice for mismanagements in their province, or to make them refund to the injured people the wealth raised by their extortions." Everywhere governors were judged and found wanting, not wholly because of what they did, but because of what they were likely to be, men of slight fortune and strangers. Benjamin Franklin summed up a century of colonial resentment when he explained to a London audience in 1768 that colonial governors were:

not like Princes whose posterity have an inheritance in the government of a nation, and therefore an interest in its prosperity; they are generally strangers to the Provinces they are sent to govern, have no estate, natural connexion, or relation there, to give them an affection for the country, ... they come only to make money as fast as they can; are sometimes men of vicious characters and broken fortunes ... as they intend staying in the country no longer than their government continues and purpose to leave no family behind them, they are apt to be regardless of the good will of the people. ...

It was this kind of corruption, believed to be operating everywhere, that moved assemblies in all the colonies to hedge about their treasuries with every device possible to stop bribery, extortion, and embezzlement. The New York assembly in 1749 frankly explained why they insisted on the control of public funds. Governors were:

generally entire strangers to the People they are sent to govern; they seldom have any Estates ... where they are appointed Governors, and consequently their Interest is entirely distinct ... they seldom regard the Welfare of the People, otherwise than as they can make it subservient to their own particular interest; and as they know the Time of the Continuance in their Governments to be uncertain, all Methods are used, and all Engines set to work to raise Estates to themselves and therefore should the public Monies be left to their Disposition, what can be expected but the grossest mis-application?

It was the corruptions of "necessitous and rapacious governors," Thomas Pownall saw after broad experience in the colonies, which compelled the assemblies to insist on annual salaries as the only "measure left to them, to prevent the misapplications of public money." Pownall said there were just "Two great points which the Colonists labour to establish": the exercise of their rights and privileges as Englishmen, and the "keeping in their own hands, the command of the revenue, and the pay of the officers of government; as a security for the conduct of those officers towards them."[34]

Pownall was quite right to make the exercise of English rights and privileges one of his two great points. The colonists prized the Constitution and the liberties secured by charters and commissions. But neither the legalistic cast of their minds nor even that powerful urge to model their governments after Parliament fully explain the relentless determination to guard their privileges. They fought so stubbornly because they knew the corruptions of power. The pledges of loyalty, the reverence for authority, the appeals for harmony, while truly representing one part of the colonists' mind, did not blind them to the depravities of human nature. They knew officials would give way to their avarice, all officials, elected and appointed, native and alien, but especially those typically indigent and detached governors who crossed the ocean to rule the colonies and seek their fortune at one and the same time. It was that perception of power, those animosities and fears pulsing below the surface of the constitutional disputes, that compelled the assemblies to defend and enlarge their privileges.[35]

Judging from Massachusetts before 1740, colonial politics were not an imitation in miniature of English politics. The categories of analysis, to be sure, were all British. Americans strove for the same liberties and were alert for the same deficiencies in government. Had royal governors exercised influence over legislators after the fashion of the British ministry, Americans would have objected after the fashion of radical Whigs. Where the governors had the patronage, those very complaints were heard; where the governors were limited, charges were infrequent and impotent. The provincial setting of American politics subdued that issue and amplified others. Because of peculiar colonial conditions legislators were less easily corrupted and less was heard of influence. But because of the relationship of the provinces to the mother country within the British system of patronage, colonial governors consistently lacked qualities that Englishmen valued in their rulers: eminence and attachment by property and family to the area they governed. These deficiencies magnified in colonial minds the dangers of avarice among royal officials and gave colonial politics their characteristic categories of explanation.

As the colonies were drawn more fully into imperial affairs after 1750, the provincial view of corruption expanded in meaning. Under the tutelage of English radicals, a growing number of colonial politicians came to see that they were part of a struggle extending beyond their own mercenary governors and their pendant tools and creatures. The ministry at home had much deeper and more malevolent designs on liberty and, in pursuit of its object, had devised methods for overreaching the restraints on power which Parliament imposed. As experience with Parliament made that idea a reality for Americans, the word "corruption" attained the fullness of meaning in colonial politics that it had long had among English radicals. It grew from simple greed to include corruption of the legislature through patronage and electoral influence and thus came to threaten the entire destruction of the Constitution.[36]

By the time the revolutionary movement came to a climax in 1776 it was deeply enmeshed in and respondent to the corresponding English movement to reform Parliament which reached its own penultimate climax in the early 1780's. In a sense the American Revolution was the extension of a conflict over legislative corruption waged in England. But in another sense the Revolution never outgrew its origins in provincial politics with provincial emphasis on corruption as sheer greed. Events after 1763 cast before the public example after example of officials defrauding the people under the guise of royal appointment: the stamp distributors, Americans themselves who betrayed their country to enjoy the profits of an oppressive office; customs commissioners, a horde of indigent strangers, smaller versions of the royal governors descending on the colonies "like dogs of prey thirsting after the fortunes of worthy and wealthy men"; and Thomas Hutchinson, monopolizing offices for the benefit of his relatives, growing fat from the fees of their multiple judgeships. The colonists came to believe that they would never be safe from the ravages of official greed so long as all appointments originated abroad and inevitably included men lacking interested attachments to the colonies. John Adams said that a "whole government of our choice, managed by persons whom we love, revere, and can confide in has charms in it for which men will fight." And fight they did, not just to escape the dominion of an oppressive ministry and a corrupted Parliament but to create a government of men they could trust, men whose interests mingled with their own and whose lust was checked by all the limitations on power enlightenment thinkers had devised. Under that government, they could at last, as they hoped, rid themselves of the avaricious appointees who, in the minds of the colonists, had been the bane of provincial politics.[37]

Notes

[1] Charles Carroll of Carrollton, to Mr. Bradshaw, Nov. 21, 1765, Thomas Meagher Field, ed., *Unpublished Letters of Charles Carroll of Carrollton . . .* (New York, 1902), p. 97. The most vivid descriptions of corruption are in Bernard Bailyn, *The Ideological Origins of the American Revolution* (Cambridge, Harvard University Press, 1967), chap. 3; Gordon Wood, *The Creation of the American Republic, 1776–1787* (Chapel Hill, Published for the Institute of Early American History and Culture by the University of North Carolina Press, 1969), p. 34–36, 107–114; and Gordon Wood, "Republicanism as a Revolutionary Idealogy," in John R. Howe, Jr., ed., *The Role of Idealogy in the American Revolution* (New York, Holt, Rinehart, and Winston, 1970), p. 83–91. For the tension with the opposite pole of virtue and public service, see Edmund S. Morgan, "The Puritan Ethic and the American Revolution," *William and Mary Quarterly*, 3d series, 24 (1967):3–43.

[2] Charles Carroll, Sr., to William Graves, Dec. 23, 1768, *Maryland Historical Magazine*, 12 (Mar. 1917):185. The classic descriptions of influence are Sir Lewis Namier, *England in the Age of the American Revolution* (London, Macmillan and Company Limited, 1930); and *The Structure of Politics at the Accession of George III*, 2d ed. (London, Macmillan and Company Limited, 1957); and Robert Walcott, *English Politics in the Early Eighteenth Century* (Cambridge, Harvard University Press, 1956).

[3] Bernard Bailyn, *The Origins of American Politics* (New York, Alfred A. Knopf, Inc., 1968), p. 136–150, 53–56; and *Ideological Origins*, p. 35–54; David L. Jacobson, ed., *The English Libertarian Heritage* (Indianapolis, The Bobbs-Merrill Company, Inc., 1965), p. xxx–xxxi, xlviii–lvii.

[4] Jack P. Greene, "Political Mimesis: A Consideration of the Historical and Cultural Roots of Legislative Behavior in the British Colonies in the Eighteenth Century," with "A Comment" by Professor Bailyn and "Reply" by Professor Greene, *American Historical Review*, 75 (Dec. 1969):337–367; and Paul Lucas, "A Note on the Comparative Study of the Structure of Politics in Mid-Eighteenth-Century Britain and Its American Colonies," *William and Mary Quarterly*, 3d series, 28 (1971):301–309.

[5] Forty percent of the revolutionary pamphlets listed in Thomas R. Adams, *American Independence, the Growth of an Idea: A Bibliographical Study of the American Political Pamphlets Printed between 1764 and 1776 . . .* (Providence, Brown University Press, 1965), originated in Massachusetts.

[6] The issues are dealt with by the participants themselves in exchanges among governor, council, and house in *Journals of the House of Representatives of Massachusetts*, 41 vols. (Boston, 1919–71), and in letters, petitions, and addresses to British officials in *Calendar of State Papers, Colonial Series, America and West Indies*, 42 vols. (London, 1860–1953). The house journals before 1715, when publication began, are lost, but the Council Records in the Massachusetts Archives fill the gap reasonably well. The best secondary account is still John Gorham Palfrey, *History of New England from the Revolution of the Seventeenth Century* (Boston, Little, Brown, and Company, 1877), vol. 4.

⁷ *Journals of the House*, vol. 11, p. 91. The governor and council frequently charged the house with moral dereliction of some sort, but only rarely and subtly were the charges reversed.

⁸ *Ibid.*, vol. 8, p. 332. The same principle of restraint operated in those infrequent instances when assembly leaders carried the argument outside the legislative chambers and published tracts in their own cause. Elisha Cooke, the manager of the popular party in the house for over 15 years, wrote a *Just and Seasonable Vindication* in 1720 after Governor Shute negatived Cooke's election as speaker and aspersed his loyalty to the crown. After firmly but judiciously restating his position and his loyalty to His Majesty, Cooke expressed the wish "that when the next Assembly come together, there may be a good Understanding and Harmony betwixt them, every Man of one Heart and one Mind, Studying to advance those great Ends they are set for, and that none in the least Measure will aspire to lessen the Prerogative of the Crown, nor willingly come into or depart from any thing ... for lessening or abridging the Peoples Rights. ..." *Mr. Cook's Just and Seasonable Vindication: Respecting Some Affairs Transacted in a Late General Assembly at Boston* (Boston, 1720), p. 18. The same spirit pervades Cooke's *Letter to Mr. Speaker Burrill and Mr. Bridger* (Boston, 1719), and a tract by Cooke's friend and fellow-representative from Boston, Oliver Noyes, in *A Letter From a Gentleman, Containing Some Remarks upon the Several Answers given unto Mr. Colman's* ... (Boston, 1720), reprinted in Andrew McFarland Davis, ed., *Colonial Currency Reprints, 1682–1751*, vol. 2 (Boston, 1911), p. 3–17.

⁹ *Journals of the House*, vol. 3, p. 98. Even more effusive on some occasions, the house could say they "are so sincerely affected for your Excellency's personal Welfare, that they will make full and ample Provision for the Governour, according to your Station and their Ability, and earnestly contend with your Excellency, which shall exceed in the Expressions of their mutual Affections." (*Boston Gazette*, Feb. 5–12, 1739).

¹⁰ *Journals of the House*, vol. 8, p. 332; P.D.G. Thomas, *The House of Commons in the Eighteenth Century* (Oxford, Clarendon Press, 1971), p. 43–44. For the thought and tactics of the opposition, see Caroline Robbins, *The Eighteenth-Century Commonwealthman* (Cambridge, Harvard University Press, 1959); Archibald S. Foord, *His Majesty's Opposition, 1714–1830* (Oxford, Clarendon Press, 1964); Laurence Hanson, *Government and the Press, 1695–1763* (Oxford, Clarendon Press, 1936); David H. Stevens, *Party Politics and English Journalism, 1702–1742* (Wenosha, Wisc., George Banta Publishing Company, 1916).

¹¹ *New England Courant*, Sept. 11 and Oct. 9, 16, 23, and 30, 1721; May 7 and July 9, 16, and 23, 1722; *Weekly Rehearsal*, Nov. 20 and 27 and Dec. 18 and 25, 1732; Jan. 1, Feb. 5 and 19, June 4, and Aug. 27, 1733. On Feb. 5, 1733, a local writer in the *Weekly Rehearsal* argued the side of the popular party in the dispute over the house audit of expenditures, the only comment in two years on provincial issues except for reprinted official statements.

¹² *The Deploreable State of New-England* ... (London, 1708), in *Collections of the Massachusetts Historical Society*, 5th series, vol. 6 (Boston, 1879), 122; cf. 103–104, 111, 115–116, 118, 119; cf. *A Memorial Of the Present Deploreable STATE of New-England* ... (n.p., 1707), in *ibid.*, p. 39, 46. The background of the scandal is found in Palfrey, *History*, vol. 4, p. 299–311. *A Letter to an Eminent Clergy-Man* (Boston, 1721), in Davis, *Colonial Currency Reprints*, vol. 2, p. 238; cf. *Reflections upon Re-*

flections, More News from Robinson Cruso's Island (Boston, 1720), in ibid., vol. 2, p. 116–117; and A Letter from a Gentleman in Mount Hope to His Friend in Treamount (Boston, 1721), in ibid., vol. 2, p. 263. Articles on preferment and influence appeared in the Courant for Apr. 21 and 30, May 14 and 28, and Dec. 10, 1722. The quotations are from the May 14 issue and from English Advice to the Freeholders, etc, of the Province of the Massachusetts-Bay (Boston, 1722), p. 2.

13 New England Courant, Dec. 24, 1722 (on the audit of accounts) and May 14, 1722 (on the mast trees). The Courant also supported the assembly on the contested election of Paul Dudley as a representative of Sagadahoc, a minor issue: May 7 and June 4, 1722. Articles against inoculation appeared on Aug. 7, 14, 21, and 28, Nov. 6 and 27, and Dec. 18, 1721, and Jan. 8 and 15, Feb. 26, Apr. 30, and May 21, 1722. Attacks on the clergy were in the issues of Sept. 25, Nov. 6 and 21, and Dec. 4, 1721, and Jan. 8 and 22, Feb. 5 and 12, and May 14, 1722. Perry Miller, The New England Mind: From Colony to Province (Cambridge, Harvard University Press, 1953), chap. 20. English Advice, p. 2–3; Journals of the House, vol. 2, p. 359, 369. On closing down the Courant, Palfrey, History, vol. 4, p. 410; Leonard Levy, Legacy of Suppression: Freedom of Speech and Press in Early American History (Cambridge, Harvard University Press, 1960), p. 36–38; Clyde Augustus Duniway, The Development of Freedom of the Press in Massachusetts (New York, Longmans, Green, and Company, 1906), p. 97–103.

14 A Letter to the Freeholders and other Inhabitants of the Massachusetts-Bay, relating to their approaching Election of Representatives ([Newport], 1739), Advertisement.

15 All the references to corruption are cited in notes 12 and 14. The authorship of The Deploreable State has been attributed to Cotton Mather and, because of the initial A.H. at the end of the introduction, to Alexander Holmes, an English merchant trading to New England. The most likely author is Henry Ashurst, long the friend of New England and the implacable enemy of Dudley. Ashurst in 1708 was determined to have Dudley removed and could not have resisted attacking his old enemy. Although I have found no record of Ashurst confessing authorship, he was involved enough to send 200 copies to Increase Mather. Various details in The Deploreable State link the tract to Ashurst: it was dedicated to Lord Sunderland whom Ashurst later blamed for keeping Dudley in office; the initials A. H. fit Ashurst; it refers familiarly to letters from the house to Ashurst. Above all, The Deploreable State was gratuitously laudatory of that "Honourable Friend of New-England, and of all Good Men, Sir Henry Ashurst." Ashurst always felt that New England was niggardly in its appreciation of his services. For earlier attributions, Collections of the Massachusetts Historical Society, 5th series, vol. 6, p. 30. On Ashurst's involvement with the pamphlet, ibid., 6th series, vol. 5 (Boston, 1892), 173, 215–217. On his hatred of Dudley, ibid., 88–92, 100, 109–110, 119, 131–132, 136, 138. On his feeling of being New England's chief defender and of being undervalued for his services, ibid., 84–85, 89–91, 109, 138, 174–175, 195–196, 199, 214, 215–216, 217–221. The praise of Ashurst is in The Deploreable State, p. 115, 117–118, 125. For the complaints of Massachusetts men, A Memorial of the Present State, p. 40–43; The Deploreable State, p. 107–108.

16 Jacobson, ed., English Libertarian Heritage, p. 126; New England Courant, May 14, 1722. On the difficulties of corruption in the colonies generally, Bailyn, Origins of

American Politics, p. 71–91; on Massachusetts, Robert E. Brown, *Middle-Class Democracy and the Revolution in Massachusetts, 1691–1780* (Ithaca, N.Y., Cornell University Press, 1955), chaps. 2, 3, 4.

[17] After adamantly opposing the governor for four years on his right to veto their speaker and their own right to dismiss themselves, the house accepted an explanatory charter from the crown which ruled against them on both counts. In the rollcall on accepting the charter, military officers and justices of the peace constituted three-fifths of the ayes and only one-fifth of the nays. But since the governor was in England and in no position to threaten them, the vote probably measured a general attitude toward royal government rather than a response to immediate political pressure. The pressure certainly did not work before 1726, when the house registered near-unanimous votes against the governor. Voters seemingly did not blame the representatives' acquiescence on the timidity of placemen, for in the 1727 election the percentage of officials in the house went up from 39 percent to 44 percent. The representatives who voted for were returned in about the same proportion as those who voted against. *Journals of the House*, vol. 6, p. 458–459; *Acts and Resolves, Public and Private, of the Province of the Massachusetts Bay* ... vol. 10 (Boston, 1902), p. 574–575; vol. 11 (Boston, 1903), p. 4–5.

In a 1739 rollcall on pulling in bills of credit by 1742, a measure Governor Belcher strongly desired, 14 justices of the peace supported him and 10 opposed along with 13 military officers. The justices on the governor's side were a far larger portion of the affirmative (14 of 19) than appointed officials were of the negative (23 of 58), but the split shows, nonetheless, that appointees were not in the governor's vest pocket. *Journals of the House*, vol. 16, p. 257–258; *Acts and Resolves*, vol. 12 (Boston, 1904), p. 566–567.

[18] From 1711 to 1740, 41 percent of the house on the average bore a military title or were called esquire, indicating an appointment as justice of the peace. The high was 60 percent, in 1735, and the low 26 percent, in 1721. The electorate presumably had no fears of placemen. The governor could not possibly have kept up had the voters chosen to avoid appointed officials. From 1711 to 1740 Middlesex County elected on the average 21 representatives each year, while the governor appointed three justices annually. *Acts and Resolves*, vols. 9–12; William H. Whitmore, ed., *The Massachusetts Civil List for the Colonial and Provincial Periods, 1630–1774* (Baltimore, Genealogical Publishing Company, 1969), p. 136–138. John Murrin makes the argument for increasing patronage power in "Essay Review," *History and Theory*, vol. 11 (1972), p. 260–261, 269–270. On the eventual agitation for a place bill in 1764, see Ellen E. Brennan, *Plural Office-Holding in Massachusetts, 1760–1780* ... (Chapel Hill, University of North Carolina Press, 1945), p. 71–73.

[19] Bailyn, *Ideological Origins*, p. 83–85, 88, 91.

[20] Thomas Bridge, in a sermon on the subject preached while the case of the illicit French trade was still being discussed, defined covetousness as "a distemper of the Soul, which manifests itself in a constant, greedy, insatiable desire after Riches, and employeth the whole man in various methods to gratifie that desire." *Jethro's Advice Recommended to the Inhabitants of Boston, in New England, viz. To Chuse Well-qualified Men, and Haters of Covetousness, for Town Officers* (Boston, 1710), p. 13.

[21] William H. Whitmore, *The Andros Tracts* . . . vol. 1 (Boston, 1868), p. 13–15; *The Plain Case Stated* (Boston, 1689), cited in T. H. Breen, *The Character of the Good Ruler: Puritan Political Ideas in New England, 1630–1730* (New Haven, Yale University Press, 1970), p. 156. Cf. *Andros Tracts*, vol. 1, p. 80, 87, 98, 114–116, 124–215, 137–138, 145; vol. 2, p. 6–7, 36, 56, 128, 192, 241–242, 247, 254–255; vol. 3, p. 195, 197–198. The memory of the depredations under Andros lingered on: *The Deploreable State*, p. 103–106.

[22] *The Deploreable State*, p. 112–113; Cotton Mather to Joseph Dudley, Boston, Jan. 21, 1708, *Collections of the Massachusetts Historical Society*, 1st series, vol. 3 (Boston, 1810), p. 130; cf. Increase's comment on the same occasion, *ibid.*, p. 126–128; Samuel Sewall, *Diary*, in *ibid.*, 5th series, vol. 6, p. 208, 213–214, 224, 228; *Boston News-Letter*, Dec. 1, 1707. The memorial from New England was reprinted in *The Deploreable State*, p. 107. *A Memorial of the Present Deploreable State*, p. 36, 40, 43, 52–53, 57, and *The Deploreable State*, p. 103–106, 108, 122; Sewall, *Diary*, p. 353; Palfrey, *History*, vol. 4, p. 322.

[23] *A Letter From One in Boston, To his Friend in the Country* (Boston, 1714), in Davis, *Colonial Currency Reprints*, vol. 1, p. 279; cf. Paul Dudley, *Objections to the Bank of Credit* . . . (Boston, 1714), in *ibid.*, vol. 1, p. 257–258. Elisha Cooke, *Letter to Mr. Speaker Burrill and Mr. Bridger*, p. 4, 9; Cooke, *Elisha Cooke's Just and Season-able Vindication*, p. 6; cf. *Journals of the House*, vol. 2, p. 220. Petition of Francis Wilks and Jonathan Belcher, 1729, *Calendar of State Papers, Colonial, 1728–1729*, p. 489. Burnet had been issuing illegal let passes for which he charged a fee. (*Ibid.*, 512)

[24] On Cooke's involvement in the private bank in 1714, Thomas Hutchinson, *The History of the Colony and Province of Massachusetts-Bay*, ed. Lawrence Shaw Mayo (Cambridge, Harvard University Press, 1936), vol. 2, p. 155; G. B. Warden, *Boston, 1689–1776* (Boston, Little, Brown, and Company, 1970), p. 69–73.

[25] *The Acts and Resolves*, vol. 1, p. 170; entries for July 16, 22, and 23, 1703, Court Records, 1699–1703 (Microfilm, Massachusetts Archives), vol. 7, p. 416, 418; Everett Kimball, *The Public Life of Joseph Dudley: A Study of the Colonial Policy of the Stuarts in New England, 1660–1715* (New York, Longmans, Green, and Company, 1911), p. 91.

[26] *The Case of the Muster Rolls of His Majesty's Castle William* . . . (Boston, 1720); *Journals of the House*, vol. 3, p. 77, 188; vol. 4, p. 161, 179; vol. 5, p. 46, 62, 69, 75–76, 82, 84, 90–93, 177, 282, 294, 328–329; vol. 6, p. 39, 58, 319–320, 330, 331, 334, 436–438; *Acts and Resolves*, vol. 10, p. 96; cf. vol. 10, p. 61–62, 134, 191, 263–264, 271, 323, 418, 454, 528; William Dummer to Newcastle, 1729, *Calendar of State Papers, Colonial, 1728–1729*, p. 495; Francis Wilks and Jonathan Belcher to the King, 1729, *ibid.*, p. 491; William Burnet to the Board of Trade, 1729, *ibid.*, p. 341; Order of Privy Council, Oct. 23, 1729, *ibid.*, p. 512–513; Draught of additional instructions to William Dummer, Nov. 12, 1729, *ibid.*, p. 524–525; Palfrey, *History*, vol. 4, p. 541, 543, 545; *Journals of the House*, vol. 11, p. 43, 50–52, 84–88, 121, 129, 142, 143, 171–172. The long quoted passage is from *Journals of the House*, vol. 11, p. 112. For a newspaper comment, see *Weekly Rehearsal*, Feb. 5, 1733. It was during this episode that the house bluntly repudiated its obligation to conform to royal instructions. *Journals of the House*, vol. 11, p. 64–68, 104.

[27] *Journals of the House*, vol. 11, p. 278; vol. 12, p. 170; vol. 17, p. vii, 81; Palfrey, *History*, vol. 4, p. 553.

[28] Henry Horwitz, "The Structure of Parliamentary Politics," in Geoffrey Holmes, ed., *Britain after the Glorious Revolution, 1689–1714* (London, Macmillan and Company, 1969), p. 106–107; *Journals of the House*, vol. 11, p. 24, 25, 277; Order of Committee of the Privy Council, Oct. 23, 1729, *Calendar of State Papers, Colonial, 1728–1729*, p. 512–513.

[29] Thomas Hutchinson said that Dudley was believed guilty of "gross bribery and corruption," but that the charges were not well founded. (*History*, vol. 2, p. 160).

[30] Thomas Pownall, *The Administration of the British Colonies*, 5th edition (London, 1774), p. 30; *The Humble Address of the Publicans of New-England* . . . (London, 1691); *Andros Tracts*, vol. 2, p. 254; Jeremiah Dummer, *A Defence of the New England Charters* (London, 1721), p. 67–68, 71. By royal instruction, appointees to office were to be men "of good Estates and Abilities, and not necessitous Persons." Charles Henry Lincoln, ed., *Correspondence of William Shirley* . . . (New York, 1912), vol. 1, p. 145; cf. Kimball, *Dudley*, p. 80.
William Douglass, who seemed eager to help Governor Burnet maximize the profits of office, reported that "Gov. Shute did make of his government three thousand pounds per annum; by management it may be doubled." There were few places of "any considerable profit," but "a great many small farms:" the naval office, the captaincies of Castle William and three smaller forts, county sheriffs, and registers of probate. "The governor has also the negativing of treasurers, commisaries of provisions and stores, impost officers, and collectors of excise, which may be managed with fellow feeling." Douglass to Cadwallader Colden, Boston, Nov. 20, 1727, *Collections of the Massachusetts Historical Society*, 4th series, vol. 2 (Boston, 1854), p. 176–177. Twenty years earlier, Cotton Mather accused Dudley of claiming that the perquisites of government in Massachusetts were worth £1200 a year. Cotton Mather to Joseph Dudley, Boston, Jan. 20, 1708, *ibid.*, 1st series, vol. 3, p. 130. For the motives and fortunes of colonial governors generally, but particularly in New York, see Beverly McAnear, *The Income of the Colonial Governors of British North America* (New York, Pageant Press Inc., 1967).

[31] William Douglass, *A Summary, Historical and Political of the First Planting, Progressive Improvements, and Present State of the British Settlements in North-America* (Boston, 1755), vol. 1, p. 481. The one good thing that could be said of Dudley by the author of *The Deploreable State* was that the governor's family and interest were in Massachusetts (p. 104). Dudley made the same point to the General Court. Palfrey, *History*, vol. 4, p. 308n. Cotton Mather, *Magnalia Christi Americana: Or, the Ecclesiastical History of New England* (Hartford, 1855), vol. 1, p. 176; Hutchinson, *History*, vol. 2, p. 175; cf. *Andros Tracts*, vol. 1, p. 13, 137–138. Boston valued its local magistrates because they were "Inhabitants of it" with "Considerable Estates in it." *My Son fear thou the Lord* (Boston, 1714), in *Publications of the Colonial Society of Massachusetts, Transactions, 1904–1906*, vol. 10 (Boston, 1907), p. 350.

[32] *Journals of the House*, vol. 8, p. 279–280; Council of Trade and Plantations to the Duke of Newcastle, Mar. 27, 1729, *Calendar of State Papers, Colonial, 1728–1729*, p. 338; Address of the House of Representatives to the King, Nov. 22, 1728, *ibid.*, p. 311–312.

[33] Not that every colony's history paralleled Massachusetts' in every respect. There was for a brief span at least one bona fide opposition press, the *New York Weekly Journal*, Zenger's publication, and there were place bills and instances of electoral influence; but they were more often overshadowed by the pervasive fear of official avarice. Bailyn, *Origins of American Politics*, p. 78–80; Stanley Nider Katz, *Newcastle's New York: Anglo-American Politics, 1732–1753* (Cambridge, Harvard University Press, 1968), p. 74–77, 83–84, 157; James Alexander, *A Brief Narrative of the Case and Trial of John Peter Zenger . . .*, ed. Stanley Nider Katz (Cambridge, Harvard University Press, 1963), Introduction.

[34] Louis B. Wright, ed., *An Essay upon the Government of the English Plantations on the Continent of America (1701)* (San Marino, Calif., 1945), p. 21; cf. p. 37; (Edmund Burke), *An Account of the European Settlements in America*, 6th ed. (London, 1777), vol. 2, p. 302; Albert H. Smyth, ed., *The Writings of Benjamin Franklin*, vol. 5 (New York, 1906), p. 83. The statement of the New York Assembly is quoted in John F. Burns, *Controversies Between Royal Governors and Their Assemblies in the Northern American Colonies* (New York, Russell and Russell, 1969), p. 21; Pownall, *Administration*, p. 69, 80–81.

In a letter to William Shirley, Dec. 4, 1754, Franklin argued that mobilization of provision and men for defense could not be safely left to governors and their councils. The main reasons were:

> That Governors often come to the Colonies merely to make Fortunes, with which they intend to return to Britain, are not always Men of the best Abilities and Integrity, have no Estates here, nor any natural Connections with us that should make them heartily concern'd for our Welfare; and might possibly be sometimes fond of raising and keeping up more Forces than necessary, from the Profits accruing to themselves and to make Provision for their Friends and Dependants. That the Councellors in most of the Colonies, being appointed by the Crown, on the Recommendation of Governours, are often of small Estates, frequently Dependant on the Governor for Offices, and therefore too much under Influence. (Lincoln, *Correspondence of William Shirley*, vol. 2, p. 103–104)

[35] The *Essay upon the Government* of 1701 vigorously argued against enlargement of the governor's powers in Virginia precisely because officials would use their authority to enhance profits. (p. 20–21)

[36] A Boston pamphleteer in 1742 who had been made aware that there were "too great a Number of Placemen and Pensioners sitting in Parliament," was happy that there were "not a great many Posts of Profit among us." But drawing a lesson from the mother country, he urged Massachusetts "to look about us, and inquire, if there have been any such among us, who have been influenced by Posts of Honour and Profit, to vote, and act too much as Men in Power would have them?" (*Boston Evening Post*, May 10, 1742.) Thus did Americans, as they were absorbed into British politics, learn to construe their own political life.

37 For American responses to reform movements in England, see Pauline Maier, *From Resistance to Revolution: Colonial Radicals and the Development of American Opposition to Britain, 1765–1776* (New York, Alfred A. Knopf, 1972), chap. 6. The indictment of customs officials is from Oliver M. Dickerson, *The Navigation Acts and the American Revolution* (Philadelphia, University of Pennsylvania Press, 1951), p. 230. The Adams quotation is in John C. Miller, *Triumph of Freedom, 1775–1783* (Boston, Little, Brown, and Company, 1948), p. 343.

Edmund S. Morgan received his B.A. and Ph.D. degrees from Harvard University. He was employed during World War II as an instrumentmaker at the Massachusetts Institute of Technology and in 1945 joined the faculty of the University of Chicago. The following year he accepted an appointment at Brown University, where he also served for a time as acting dean of the graduate school. In 1955 Professor Morgan began teaching at Yale, and in 1965 he was named Sterling Professor of History, the position he holds today. He is also a member of the advisory committee of the Library of Congress American Revolution Bicentennial Program.

Professor Morgan's publications include The Puritan Family *(1944, 1966),* The Stamp Act Crisis *(with Helen Morgan, 1953, 1963),* The Birth of the Republic *(1956),* The Puritan Dilemma *(1958),* The Gentle Puritan *(1962),* Visible Saints *(1963), and* Roger Williams; The Church and State *(1967).*

As MUCH AT HOME with the Puritans as with the Founding Fathers, with a John Winthrop or a Roger Williams as with an Ezra Stiles, covering with equal distinction and competence the two quite diverse centuries of American colonial experience is Edmund S. Morgan, who comments on Professor Bushman's paper.

Royal and Republican Corruption

EDMUND S. MORGAN

PROFESSOR BUSHMAN HAS PRESENTED US with a new view of prerevolutionary political attitudes that conditioned American reactions to British authority in the revolutionary era. That Americans saw the British government as corrupt is well known. That they feared corruption in their own governments is also well known. But we have not hitherto been shown the distinctions that Professor Bushman has so lucidly set forth in what Americans meant by corruption. The colonists, he explains, did not, before the revolutionary era, think of corruption as a threat posed by the executive to the integrity and independence of their legislative assemblies. Rather, the threat of corruption lay in the simple avarice of the executive, that is, in the royal governor's presumed disposition to use his office as a means of obtaining wealth. The source of the threat, as the colonists saw it, lay partly in the poverty of those who held the office of governor, and partly in the fact that they were usually aliens, without attachments or interests in the society that they governed.

Professor Bushman has presented abundant evidence that these ideas about corruption prevailed among the colonists before the revolutionary period. And he suggests that the colonists reached their views in reaction against the sorry lot of well-to-do British paupers whom the king sent to govern them. Perhaps. But if experience taught them to want wealthy governors and governors chosen from their own ranks, then they were singularly obtuse or perverse in what they chose to learn from experience.

As Professor Bushman observes, one of the primary devices of the colonial legislatures in trying to control the executive was the annual salary. By keeping the governor economically dependent they could set limits to his avarice. But was it only his avarice that they wished to control through their annual appropriations? Could they not see that a wealthy governor would have had economic independence and would not have been as easily kept in line by limitation to an annual salary? The experience of other colonists, particularly the Virginians, suggested that a rich governor might be even more eager for the spoils of office than a poor one. The rich frequently show more interest in getting rich than the poor do. And if the colonists of Massachusetts yearned for a governor chosen from their own ranks, they must have had a very short memory of their experience with Gov. Joseph Dudley, son of one of the founders of the colony, not to mention their later experience in the revolutionary period with Thomas Hutchinson, also a native and a descendant of first settlers. Dudley and Hutchinson were the two most unpopular governors of Massachusetts in the 18th century; William Shirley, an alien, was probably the most popular. I bring up these contradictions not to cast doubt on the validity of Professor Bushman's analysis of colonial attitudes toward corruption but merely to suggest that the attitudes seem doctrinaire, growing perhaps as much from theology or political philosophy or provincial snobbery as from experience.

I would like to suggest also that the transformation during the revolutionary period of American attitudes toward corruption was not confined (as I am sure Professor Bushman would agree) to the new fear of executive corruption of the legislature brought on by the contest with a corrupted Parliament. After the Declaration of Independence the danger of corruption from alien rulers was removed, and in the ensuing years Americans had opportunities to learn about legislative corruption close to home. The Continental Congress was in no danger of corruption by the executive power because there was no continental executive power, alien or native. Yet the Congress lost no time in demonstrating its vulnerability to vice. In the financial maneuvers of Robert Morris and in the operations of the various land companies among the members it was not difficult to detect avarice, both simple and not so simple. By 1779 Richard Henry Lee, who had offered the resolution that declared American independence, was writing to George Mason that "the demon of avarice, extortion, and fortune-making seizes all ranks. And now, to get into office is another thing for getting into wealth on public funds and to the public injury."[1] Henry Laurens, President of the Congress, thought that the country abounded "with practices of peculation and sacrilegious Robberies of public Money."[2] The fever afflicted the state governments as much as Congress; the financial measures by which the state legislators met the expenses of government seemed designed to defraud creditors and enrich speculators, among whom were numbered many of the legislators.

The Americans did not have to formulate a new political philosophy to explain this kind of legislative corruption. In the writings of the 18th-century commonwealthmen, which Caroline Robbins has identified and described and from which the colonists had learned their republican lessons, they could find plenty of warning against the special dangers of corruption in a republic. In a monarchy like England the source of corruption might be a king who bribed the legislators with places and profits. But in a republic, the commonwealthmen made plain, the source of corruption or of resistance to corruption lay in the people themselves, because in a republic the people were sovereign. The success of a republic depended on the widespread diffusion among them of property on the one hand and of virtue on the other. If they should lose their virtue, neither annual elections nor secret ballots would prevent them from choosing corrupt men to make their laws.

In the corruption of their legislatures, therefore, the Americans caught a glimpse of themselves, and the vision appalled them. They had betrayed their Revolution, it seemed, almost before it was over. Avarice was still the great source of corruption, but it had reached through the land and gripped the whole people. Virtue, always a fragile thing, had crumbled before its onslaughts and reduced the people to luxury and idleness. In the face of universal corruption, republican liberty could not long survive. Silas Deane, who seemed to many the embodiment of corruption, was himself convinced by 1781 that his countrymen could not sustain a republican government, because they had exchanged "plain morals and honest industry for the habits of idleness and vice."[3] And six years later, in 1787, Deane's old opponent Arthur Lee, the embodiment in his own eyes at least of virtue, was ready to admit, "it is now manifest that we have not the public virtue and private temperance which are necessary to the establishment . . . of free Republics."[4]

Lee was writing as the Philadelphia Convention gathered, and he expected no good to come of it. Those who attended, if more optimistic, would not have discounted the danger that he might be right. Their task, as they saw it, was one of nurturing virtue through a government that depended on the virtue it nurtured. The bootstrap operation was a difficult one, but worth, they thought, a try. The problem was still corruption, but they had acquired a more intimate acquaintance with its complexities than the colonists who thought that a rich native governor would be the answer to their problems. Perhaps because they had learned more about it, the men at Philadelphia succeeded, to some degree at least, in coping with it. Their solution, as every morning newspaper makes clear today, was not foolproof. But that fact would scarcely have surprised them.

Notes

[1] James C. Ballagh, ed., *The Letters of Richard Henry Lee* (New York, Macmillan, 1911), vol. 2, p. 65.

[2] Edmund C. Burnett, ed., *Letters of Members of the Continental Congress* (8 vols., Washington, The Carnegie Institution of Washington, 1921–36), vol. 3, p. 248.

[3] *Collections of the New-York Historical Society for the year 1889*, p. 350.

[4] Burton J. Hendrick, *The Lees of Virginia* (Boston, Little, Brown & Co., 1935).

Pauline R. Maier received a B.A. degree from Radcliffe College and a Ph.D. degree from Harvard University. She also attended the London School of Economics as a Fulbright scholar. Professor Maier was a teaching fellow at Harvard in 1968, when she accepted an appointment to the Department of History at the University of Massachusetts, Boston, where she is now an associate professor. In addition to various scholarly articles, she has published a monographic study entitled From Resistance to Revolution: Colonial Radicals and the Development of American Opposition to Britain, 1765–1776 *(1972).*

CONTINUING OUR THEME for this symposium, the development of a revolutionary mentality, it is only appropriate that both of the following papers should be presented by women. Lately women seem to have been carrying the heaviest burdens of revolutionary ardor, and it is not unlikely that Abigail Adams, Mercy Otis Warren, and Catharine Macaulay would view with approval this devotion to the cause of revolution on the part of their sex. Whatever its long-range outcome, and male chauvinists are already having some misgivings, women historians have in the last few years performed scholarly work of high competence and originality in the field of the American Revolution. We are especially indebted to Pauline Maier, whose investigations of popular uprisings in 18th-century America and the impact of John Wilkes on American radical thought have opened up new and important lines of inquiry.

The Beginnings of American Republicanism 1765–1776

PAULINE MAIER

AMERICANS OF THE MID-18TH CENTURY held defined and emphatic views on government. They were "no friends to republicanism," as Charleston's Christopher Gadsden emphasized in 1763, but instead "ardent lovers" of the British Constitution, which was for them "the Work of Ages ... the Envy and Admiration of the Universe, the Glory of the English Nation." No form of government seemed so fitted for the preservation of liberty. King, Lords, and Commons shared power in a mixed structure that prevented any one of them from pursuing its own interests at the cost of the nation's freedom. Even the colonial Sons of Liberty, who organized to resist the Stamp Act in 1765 and 1766, were outspoken in their conviction of "the Superior Excellence of the English Constitution to that of any other Form of Government upon Earth." And should independence ultimately become necessary—a prospect the Sons of Liberty envisaged only with the "darkest Gloom and Horror"—they assumed that the institutions of a separate America would resemble those of the mother country, that ex-colonists would set about "erecting an Independent Monarchy here in America."[1]

These attitudes were not easily set aside, for they were part of a loyalty to Britain deeply engrained in American life. Participation in the freest system of government in the world was a source of pride, even identity, for colonists. This pervasive affection for Britain explains why independence was so reluctantly accepted. Yet as independent nationals, the Americans did not attempt simply to reduplicate the old British system. Instead they embarked upon an innovative path, which by then they were ready to call "republican." This development made the American Revolution far more than a colonial revolt: Republicanism carried implications for a widespread reformation of American politics and society. And it expanded the significance of the American revolt beyond the New World, making the Revolution a "symbol for the liberation of all mankind," an opening event in what R. R. Palmer has called "the Age of the Democratic Revolution."[2]

Republicanism also made the American Revolution a more difficult event to understand. This was true for contemporaries, who struggled to work out its meaning in the new nation; it is true, too, for modern Americans. Had colonists ceased their innovations with independence, their revolt would be easily grasped, for struggles against imperialism remain. But republicanism is today so established, so common, and the monarchical alternative against which the revolutionaries warred is so benign, that it is not easy to comprehend a time when "republican" was a term of opprobrium[3] and the espousal of republican ideology a radical achievement.

Equally puzzling is the process by which the Americans came to be "republicans." No well-known defense of republicanism as a system was made before Thomas Paine's *Common Sense*, a fact which led Cecelia Kenyon to conclude that the ideological transition occurred "in a few months" in 1776.[4] The foundations for this apparent "conversion" to republicanism were, however, well laid by the time Paine wrote. Like independence, republicanism arose from a decade of frustrating efforts to gain redress of grievances within the British system. As grievances multiplied, as the threat to liberty became increasingly manifest, the indictment of current rulers widened into an extended critique of the British system. But if the British Constitution was incapable of maintaining freedom, previous republican governments had also been flawed. Here the extralegal organizations that colonists founded to organize their resistance took on a new importance: they suggested that republicanism was viable, that it constituted a better alternative for America.

1

Technically, the word "republic" denoted less a specific form than the overall objective of government. Derived from the Latin *res publica,* it meant "the *public good,* or the good of the whole," as Paine explained, "in contradistinction to the despotic form, which makes the good of the sovereign, or of one man, the only object of the government."[5] So broad was this concept that "republicanism" became the equivalent of legitimacy; indeed, in the writings of those 18th-century Whig authors preferred by the colonists, republicanism was practically synonymous with freedom.[6] Within these terms even England's constitution could have qualified as "republican"—had it worked in fact as it did in theory, restraining the power of king, nobles, and people so that the public welfare triumphed over special interests.

The word was, however, rarely used in this sense in mid-18th-century Anglo-American politics. Instead republicanism was associated with the commonwealth period of English history—for "commonwealth" is the closest English equivalent of "republic"—when England was ruled by neither king nor lords. Thus "commonwealthman," like "republican," became a pejorative term, suggesting "in the ordinary Meaning of the Word," as Robert Molesworth testified in 1721, "*Haters* of *Kingly* Government."[7] Neither word was, however, applied with ideological precision, for not even the heirs of England's revolutionary tradition, the "18th-century commonwealthmen" studied by Caroline Robbins, were prepared to overthrow the comforts of Augustan England for the disorder that seemed to characterize all previous republican experiments, whether in ancient Rome and Greece or in England of the 1650's. A commonwealth might be admired as the ideal form of government in theory, but as for the real world, it was utopian, a better government perhaps than men were capable of receiving: "I conceive that Liberty may be better preserved by a well poised Monarchy," John Trenchard and Thomas Gordon wrote, "than by any popular Government that I know now in the World, whatever Forms may exist in Imagination." Certainly with its present distribution of property, England could "preserve Liberty by no other Establishment than what we have," and as such "the Phantome of a Commonwealth must vanish, and never appear again but in disordered Brains." The efforts of most commonwealthmen or "Old Whigs" in the 18th century were, accordingly, geared toward protecting or "restoring" the British constitution.[8]

It was, then, the continuation of hereditary rule, particularly monarchy, that distinguished English government from a commonwealth. And the firmness with which Americans like Gadsden renounced republicanism in the early 1760's followed logically from their attachment to the British crown, which, they argued, was distinctive among European monarchies. Like their allies in England, colonists stressed that George III was of the "Illustrious House of Hanover," which owed its right to rule to the Glorious Revolution of 1688; he was heir to the "Protestant Succession" that replaced the tyranny of James II, a Catholic. The Hanoverians made no claim to absolute power but consented to rule under law and within the restraints imposed by the revolutionary settlement which, it was said, had rebalanced the constitution. George III was, moreover, the first Hanoverian to be born in England; he told his people that he gloried in the name of Briton and began his reign determined to purify England of the political "corruption" that seemed a portent of doom for English freedom to left-leaning observers. Clearly *"he glories in being King of freemen, and not of slaves,"* a writer in the American *Constitutional Courant* (1766) declared; and as such the Sons of Liberty could claim that they resisted the Stamp Act from "Principles of true Loyalty to his Majesty."[9]

Within the next decade these attitudes gradually decayed. Indeed, the development of the American Revolution is in part a history of disillusionment with the king. So late as 1767 George III remained the "darling of America." Attitudes changed slowly and in response to a series of events, starting with his condemnation of Massachusetts leaders in November 1768, becoming more serious when he rejected a series of petitions for redress from England, America, and Ireland in 1769 and the early 1770's, and intensifying in 1774 when he assented to the Intolerable Acts. This increasing indictment of George III, the identification of him with classical tyrants like Nero or with the Stuart "despots," was in itself of great significance, for the king was a symbolic embodiment of the state. When he ceased to be above party, the controversy took on revolutionary overtones.[10]

Progressive disillusionment with George III was, moreover, coupled with a developing argument against monarchy as an institution, an argument that by 1776 included all the major considerations brought together by

Paine in *Common Sense*. In September 1770 the Massachusetts Assembly heard a sermon on the ninth chapter of Nehemiah:

Behold, we are Servants this day, and for the Land that thou gavest unto our fathers, to eat the fruit thereof, and the good thereof, behold we are Servants in it. And it yieldeth much increase unto the Kings *whom thou hast set over us because of our Sins*: also they have dominion over our bodies, and over our Cattle, at their pleasure and we are in great distress.

The text, William Palfrey wrote, was "a Sermon in itself." Thereafter American writers continued to elaborate the argument that kings represented blights, not blessings. Two years before the outbreak of war, readers of the *Massachusetts Spy* were told by "A REPUBLICAN" that "Kings have been a curse to this and every other country where they have gained a footing;" of all men "Kings ... are the least to be trusted." Unless "under such an *excellent* King as the *present*," he suggested with sarcasm, "every man of sense and independency" would prefer a "well constructed REPUBLIC" to a monarchy. A September 1775 commencement speaker at Princeton, N.J., made the same point by citing all the reigning monarchies—Sweden, Turkey, Russia, Prussia, France, Spain, and Portugal; even England, it seemed, had become "the land of slavery—the school of paricides and the nurse of tyrants." Indeed, the orator concluded, "the history of Kings and Emperors is little more than the history of royal villany. The supreme governor of the universe seems to have set up arbitrary Princes on purpose to shew us the concentrated depravity of the human heart." Little wonder, then, that clergymen continually sought God's blessing on the king, since "the wickedest of men stand most in need of prayer."[11]

The combination of a debased and selfish human nature with the "trappings of monarchy," in Milton's phrase, seemed peculiarly suited to produce tyranny. "Kings are but men, ... subject to all the passions of human nature," a 1774 article in the *New London Gazette* pointed out; thus they were "too prompt to grasp at arbitrary power, and to wish to make all things bend and submit to their will and pleasure."[12] Their lofty situation fed this lust, as "Monitor" [Arthur Lee] explained in the January 25, 1776, *New York Journal*. "Their being educated in a taste for luxury, magnificence and pleasure, and surrounded with a great tribe of favourites, flatterers, and sycophants, powerfully inclines them to rapaciousness."

To some degree these circumstances affected all hereditary office, which represented for Lee, among others, "an absurdity" because it guaranteed "that a vitious or immeritorious Son ... enjoy that distinction and those privileges ... given to the virtue and merit of his Father," which was "at once preposterous and pernicious." "The experience of all times and states has proved," he argued in 1775, that nobles and patricians held ideas "dangerous to the Community," that they "always view the rights of the People with a malignant eye, and employ their power and influence to subvert them." And since kings were particularly pampered, "open to all the temptations the most formidable to frail humanity," it was "reasonable to expect that they would be oftener vicious than virtuous"—a conclusion that Lee found "verified by the general experience of nations." So avid became their thirst for power, an earlier writer noted, that kings were "scarcely ever to be tamed; and the only sure method of preventing their doing mischief is, to muzzle them or draw their talons."[13]

Monarchy, in short, was a poor risk. "A good King is a miracle," a writer in the *Pennsylvania Packet* concluded in late 1774; and at the 1775 commencement in Princeton it was said that only God could be entrusted with kingly power, for "it requires the wisdom, the goodness, and all the other attributes of a Deity to support it." Certainly public advantages had been won from kings, even aside from the "vast increase of debt and taxes" that the "REPUBLICAN" of 1773 had called the only gift of monarchy. But these "signal benefits" were inadvertent, even "contrary to [the kings'] own intention:"[14]

To John's oppressions, and Henry the Third's weakness, we owe the two great charters. To Henry the Eighth we are indebted for our freedom from the power of the Court of Rome, and the Pope's supremacy. To James and Charles the First we are beholden for the petition of right; And lastly to James the Second's bigotry we must place the settlement of the revolution.

As of 1765 England's postrevolutionary kings, especially the Hanoverians, seemed to offer an exception to the dismal history of royalty; but 10 years later it was said that William III could be "censured with as little ceremony as James the First, and his three immediate successors were all of them enemies of the people of England." Even the limited power granted the monarchs after 1688 had proved too much, and they, too, fitted the pattern of English dynastic pretensions as outlined by a writer in 1774. Only rarely did the crown descend in a regular manner for more than three generations, he claimed, probably because a dynasty that held the crown over three successions "increased their power to such a great degree as to be obnoxious to the people, and dangerous to their constitution, rights, and liberties." No longer did it seem fitting to cite the Glorious Revolution as the source of Hanoverian rule. Instead the common ancestry of Stuarts and Hanoverians was stressed. Both descended from William the Conquerer, who was, as an article of 1774 said, "a SON OF A WHORE." "A French bastard landing with an armed banditti, and establishing himself king of England against the consent of the natives," Thomas Paine later observed, "is in plain terms a very paltry rascally original." The nefarious tendency of monarchy thus became universal through history; there were no more exceptions.[15]

2

When liberty proved no safer under a Hanoverian king than a Stuart, in England than in France or Denmark, the efficacy of the British Constitution was naturally brought into question. There was little place in 18th-century Whig thought for any intrinsic reverential quality in government: institutions were judged by their performance. Government was "a mere Piece of Clock-Work," with "Springs and Wheels" that had to be arranged so the mechanism would "move to the publick Advantage." For a time the British Constitution had seemed the consummate achievement of political engineering; but in the course of the Anglo-American conflict it proved instead, as Paine put it, "imperfect, subject to convulsions, and incapable of producing what it seems to promise." Already in December 1773 Newport's Ezra Stiles found his "Ideas of the Eng[lish] Constitution ...much diminished." It no longer seemed a well-poised arrangement of king, Lords, and Commons, but instead "a kind of fortuitous consolida[tion] of Powers now in Opposition to the true Interest of the people." So fundamental was the disorder that efforts to "patch up" or restore this "broken Constitution" seemed "almost as discouraging as to essay the Recovery of an hydrop[si]cal Subject which with many Excellencies in it carries about it the seeds of inevitable Death." Suddenly it seemed that "England has been struggling under Disease for ages. It has at Times and in some parts received a temporary Cure—but the Disorder is so radically seated as will at last baffle every political physician." Devotion became an "obstinate prejudice" from which Americans must be freed: "as a man, who is attached to a prostitute, is unfitted to choose or judge a wife," Paine wrote, "so any prepossession in favour of a rotten constitution of government will disable us from discerning a good one."[16]

Britain's failure meant that enlightened legislatures had to return to the task of rearranging, even manufacturing anew, the wheels and springs of government. Discussion of new institutional forms first arose, in fact, with Corsica in mind. Pascal Paoli, who led the Corsicans' fight for independence, asked Jean Jacques Rousseau to design one for him. Catharine Macaulay interested herself in the problem and published her own scheme, then added in a second edition (1769) a letter of criticism from an unnamed American gentleman. After Corsica's fall Ezra Stiles tried his hand at designing a new constitution for England; but ultimately the constitutionalists' efforts centered on America, which because of Britain's degeneration most urgently needed new institutions.[17]

Stiles hoped that the "Men of Genius and penetrat[in]g Observation" who took up the task of replacing "old, injudiciously formed and decayed Governments" would "take a large and comprehensive View of the politics of the States and Countries around the Globe," considering not only insights from Greece, Rome, and England, but also those "of Orientals and Asiatics, of the World itself both in ancient and modern Ages." Inevitably, however, Americans dwelled more on the familiar British Constitution, seeking to retain its remaining "excellencies" and eliminate its "hydropsical" elements. As the colonies seemed "striding fast to independence" in April 1774, North Carolina's William Hooper predicted they would soon adopt Britain's Constitution "purged of its impurities, and from an experience of its defects guard against those evils which have wasted its vigor and brought it to an untimely end." And in England a year later Brand Hollis, too, hoped that the Americans, "knowing the errors of England," would avoid them, "fix their Liberties on a solid basis and . . . show to the world a perfect form of Government where Liberty and Justice shall act in Union."[18]

By 1775 many were ready to argue that monarchy was the major error of Britain's regime. But if kingly power had proven impossible to constrain and so produced "convulsions" every few generations, was the republican alternative any better? Already in 1774 loyalists accused the revolutionaries of leading America into the "maizy labyrinths of perplexity and disorder" always associated with popular governments. Even when designed by extraordinary "law-givers" like Lycurgus and Solon, republics, opponents claimed, were structurally inferior to limited monarchies: "like ill-constructed machines, set in motion, they perished by their own instability and unwieldiness." Basic to all the loyalist arguments against republics—that they were given to factionalism; that they could not be extended over a large area—was this traditional notion that "tumult and riot" were part of simple democracies unchecked by hereditary rulers. The best republics existed "only in memory," an observation which suggested that the American leaders were asking their countrymen to give up a "substance actually enjoyed, for a shadow or phantom." Like Trenchard and Gordon 50 years earlier, a writer of 1776 emphasized that a republic was utopian, "ideal, . . . a mere creature of a warm imagination."[19]

No answer to this argument was posed in 1774. Instead, defenders of the American cause denied republican partisanship and emphasized their continued hopes for an accommodation of the Anglo-American dispute within the context of Empire. If this possibility failed, and independence became unavoidable, suggestions persisted that a new, separate monarchy would be established in America: for if, as the Declaration of Independence said, prudence dictated that "Governments long established should not be changed for light and transient causes," it certainly demanded that no changes be made unless a more promising alternative existed. So late as March 5, 1775, Joseph Warren, a leading Boston radical, indicated that colonists might fix their "adored Goddess, Liberty, fast by a *Brunswick's* side, on the *American* Throne," a statement which suggested that more than military planning was involved in a recent proposal that Karl Wilhelm Ferdinand, duke of Brunswick, be invited to command the American army. The duke of Brunswick would have been an appropriate king for America, were monarchy to be retained. A relative of George III and favored nephew of Frederick the Great, the duke was a popular hero and advocate of reform who had apparently been shunned by George III and the British court in 1764, when the duke visited England to marry the Princess Augusta. In retaliation Brunswick called on William Pitt, identifying himself, like the American colonists, with the English opposition.[20]

Soon after Lexington and Concord, however, Warren abandoned any thought of an American king. In May 1775 he wrote Samuel Adams that he hoped never again to enter a political war and so wanted all the "seeds of despotism" uprooted from American institution. In particular, he asked that "the only road to promotion may be through the affection of the people"—which was, in essence, a plea for the republic. Fears that the American republic would dissolve under the force of internal disorder were not definitively overcome during the revolutionary period but persisted into the 1790's and, in altered form, down to the Civil War. By the time independence was declared, however, John Adams, like Joseph Warren, could at least hope that the "new-born" republic "might be more glorious than any former republics have been."[21]

What allowed the Americans to think they could avoid the plague of disorder that had infected all previous commonwealths? The answer, essential to the republican commitment of 1776, lay in their own experience with self-government in the revolutionary period.

Throughout the 18th century the colonists had, of course, increasingly exercised powers of self-government through their provincial assemblies, which steadily assumed powers previously held by the appointed royal governors—powers over the raising and distributing of public revenue, over their own composition, proceedings, and privileges, even over the personnel and policy of the executive branch. Jack Greene has argued that this legislative "quest for power" represented "a movement for autonomy in local affairs." In their own time, accordingly, colonists were condemned as "republicans" by royal officials. Similarly, J. R. Pole recently observed that "the American colonies developed the characteristics of what would later be known as a republican form of government many years before they were to claim to be republican in principle."[22]

Yet the provincial assemblies provided no clear paradigm for republican experiments after independence, for they acted as part of a political system conceived as a provincial model of the British Constitution, in which the governor took the place of the king, the assembly of the Commons, and the council, however imperfectly, of the House of Lords. Never was the restraining influence of the crown disputed in principle, however much royal governors were criticized and their powers curtailed. Indeed, the assemblies' efforts increased the similarity between British and provincial institutions by removing from the royal governors powers long since denied the crown "at home" and transforming themselves into "miniature Houses of Commons."[23]

A more exact precedent for the regular republican governments established from the mid-1770's lay in the associations formed to regularize colonial resistance to British legislation. Here finally there was no illusion that the people at large shared power with other more restricted estates of the realm. Resistance organizations were extralegal, irregular, and, like the Parliamentary Convention of 1689 that bridged the reigns of James II and William and Mary, were acceptable as such because they were assumed to be temporary, designed to deal with immediate but transitory problems in ways that could not be done through established governmental institutions. Within these associations, all authority was directly founded upon popular assent, in part because English revolutionary tradition taught that no resistance to government was legitimate unless it flowed from the "body of the people." Already in 1765–66 the Sons of Liberty strove to expand their base of support through all social orders; and the goal of involving the "body of the people" was continued in the nonimportation movement of

1768-79.[24] The associations founded in the southern colonies in 1769 represent a significant stage in this effort: in form those agreements were social compacts, whose authority was clearly founded upon a mutual pact of the people with each other. As such they foreshadowed a major accomplishment of the first state constitutions. The Virginia Associations of 1769 and 1770 called upon "all Gentlemen, Merchants, Traders, and other Inhabitants of this Colony" to sign their subscription lists; the rules of the association would then be "binding on all and each" of them. The Maryland Association of June 1769 began with a declaration that "We, the Subscribers, his Majesty's loyal and dutiful Subjects, the Merchants, Traders, Freeholders, Mechanics, and other Inhabitants of the Province of Maryland ... do hereby agree, and bind ourselves to, and with each other ... that we will strictly and faithfully observe, and conform to the following Resolutions." The formula was continued with appropriate modifications in the Continental Association of 1774: the original signatories, delegates to the Continental Congress, pledged that they "and the inhabitants of the several colonies, whom we represent, firmly agree and associate, under the sacred ties of virtue, honour and love of our country," to abide by the articles of the association; and again, "we do solemnly bind ourselves and our constituents ... to adhere to this association." The new nonimportation effort was, moreover, to be enforced by local committees elected by those qualified to vote in legislative elections.[25]

As the associators grew in confidence that they spoke for "the body of the people," from whom they had received a direct grant of power, they assumed a new legitimacy and authority within their limited spheres of action, becoming, in effect, microstates, or, as William Henry Drayton charged in South Carolina, a new legislative power. The tendency was already apparent by 1770, but after 1774, as the validity of British rule was increasingly disputed, new-founded committees and congresses increasingly assumed effective governmental power: "there is not a justice of the peace in Virginia that acts, except as a Committee-man," Governor Dunmore complained in December 1774. Those who refused to sign the new associations, abide by their provisions, or at least forgo public condemnations of measures "universally received and approved" were tried and, if convicted, were advertised as enemies of liberty—"Rebels against the State"—and, as the New York Provincial Congress said, "entirely put out of the protection of this Congress." Always extralegal practices were patterned after those of regularly constituted institutions: "What should we think of our honorable courts," one newspaper article of 1774 asked, "if they should punish criminals by *tar and feathers* ...?" In short, in the course of responding to changing circumstances, the resistance movement had inadvertently evolved —as the loyalists rightly recognized—into a *de facto* republican state.[26]

The associations adopted by colonists before independence were, moreover, designed specifically to contain what was considered the major danger of republican institutions—popular anarchy. This was true already in the Stamp Act crisis: the Sons of Liberty were organized only in late 1765 and on through the spring of 1766, well after November 1, 1765, when the Stamp Act had been scheduled to go into effect. By the time they emerged, then, the Stamp Act had already met active resistance. Should Britain try armed enforcement of the act, the Sons were ready to resist force with force. Lacking such challenges, however, their main preoccupation was with preventing disorder from extending beyond what was necessarily involved in resisting the Stamp Act, since excessive popular force violated accepted standards of just action and alienated supporters, weakening the popular base of resistance and making repeal of the Stamp Act less likely. The Sons of Liberty were unanimous in their resolution "to discourage and discountenance all tumultuary and riotous Proceedings, to maintain the Laws, and to preserve Peace and good Order." Words were, moreover, backed by action—either by intervening in explosive situations or by providing machinery through which the occasions of uncontrollable disorder were prevented. At Albany, N.Y., for example, subscribers to the Sons of Liberty association promised to take no action against the enemies of freedom without the advice and consent of their president and a committee of 13 whom they had chosen as officers. And then actions were to be made "in the most regular and orderly manner, aiming at nothing but the promotion and security of the GENERAL CAUSE."[27]

Likewise, nonimportation was advocated from the beginning as an alternative to "riots and tumults." To talk as if rights could be defended only by those disorderly recourses was "as much out of the way," Pennsylvania's John Dickinson stressed in calling for resistance to the Townshend Acts, "as if a man having a choice of several roads to reach his journey's end, should prefer the worst for no other reason but because it *is* the worst." "Constitutional methods of seeking Redress," particularly petitions and nonimportation, were far preferable. Americans must avoid "even the appearance of violence," Virginia's George Mason emphasized: thus the colonists relied less upon mobs than upon boycotts and social ostracism to coerce nonimportation violators, a technique that first evolved in the Stamp Act crisis and was continued on into the war years. The county conventions that sprang up in Massachusetts from July 1774 similarly sought "the discouragement of all licentiousness, and suppression of all mobs and riots," encouraging citizens to "observe the most strict obedience to all constitutional laws and authority." Continually, crowds were organized so as to limit disorder: when a mass of people assembled at Cape Cod in 1774 to prevent the meeting of the county court and to ferret out British partisans, it first adopted rules of proceeding that outlawed the intemperate use of liquor, profane language, the invasion of property, or violence "otherwise than ... shall be approved of and accounted necessary by our community for the accomplishing the errand we go upon." Individual action was not acceptable; instead patriots in the several colonies were asked to process all suspicions and complaints through their local committees.[28]

Not even the most outspoken defenders of the American cause denied that "unwarrantable excesses" had occurred. Indeed, the rash of attacks on loyalists after the outbreak of war was one reason American leaders sought the reestablishment of regular government. But was absolute and perfect order a suitable standard by which to measure the achievement of extra-legal government, given the normal level of tumultuousness in 18th-century American (and English) society, and, more important, the unusually trying circumstances of 1774–76? More appropriately Mercy Otis Warren argued that fewer incidents took place than in "any country under similar circumstances":

Witness the convulsions of Rome on the demolition of her first race of kings; the insurrections and commotions of her colonies before the downfall of the commonwealth; and to come nearer home, the confusions, the mobs, the cruelties in Britain in their civil convulsions, from William the Conquerer to the days of the Stuarts, and from the arbitrary Stuarts to the riots of London and Liverpool, even in the reign of George the third.

The "long interregnum of law and government" after the disintegration of British authority had not concluded in "riot and confusion, desolation and bloodshed." Indeed, "not a life was lost till the trump of war summoned all parties to the field."[29]

It was not just the relative absence of violence that struck observers, however, but a more general "harmony and internal peace." The years immediately before the Declaration of Independence appeared to Whigs "the great period of the Revolution," Gordon Wood has written, "the time of greatest denial and cohesion," when social relationships were remarkably free of altercation. This achievement was all the more astonishing because it was effected under institutions understood to be legitimate but yet imperfect. It was "a singular phenomenon in the story of human conduct"—

one laden with implications for the future of government—"that the rec-
ommendations of committees and conventions ... should be equally influential and binding with the severest code of law, backed by royal authority,
and strengthened by the murdering sword of despotism." Some attributed
this harmony to an extraordinary virtue in the American people, a willingness to sacrifice private convenience for the public good, that had traditionally been considered necessary for the survival of a republic. Virtue, as
understood by the Whigs, involved deference, a willingness on the part of
the "many" to be ruled, as J. G. A. Pocock has recently stressed; and
clearly American experience of the mid-1770's suggested that the people
were willing to venerate and obey not just hereditary rulers but governments entirely of their own choice, made up of men whom they could
"love, revere, and ... confide in." Fears of anarchy were now inappropriate:
the colonists' "spirit of good order and obedience to continental government" should have been "sufficient to make every reasonable person easy
and happy on that head."[30] And was internal harmony the only gain?
Paine pushed the argument further, in effect reversing traditional stereotypes. The republics of Europe, he claimed, were "always" at peace, while
monarchies engendered not only civil but foreign wars. The "pride and
insolence ever attendant on regal authority, swells into a rupture with
foreign powers, in instances, where a republican government ... would
negotiate the mistake."[31]

Given the success of America's extralegal government, a republic could
finally be defined in positive terms—no longer as simply a state without
king and lords but as a "civil society wherein the community at large takes
the care of its own welfare, and manages its concerns by representatives
elected by the people out of their own body," what Alexander Hamilton
would call a "representative democracy."[32] Now even the failures of previous republics were explicable. The "feuds, factions, and animosities" that,
along with foreign wars, constituted Roman history resulted not from the
popular character of the government of Rome but above all from the fact
that it, like the English Commonwealth, was an imperfect republic: disorder was "occasioned by the existence of a rank of nobles, whose interest
was unconnected with the plebeians" and so caused a "continual contest"
between Senate and people. A nation, one writer claimed, had to consist
of "all Kings, all nobles, or all simple freemen, to prevent such confusions,
and preserve its privileges." The notion also militated against the complex
divisions of the British Constitution. "The ever-memorable Congress now
in *America*," it was said in 1776, "has done business infinitely better than

if there had been several orders of Delegates to contest, interrupt, and be a negative one upon another."[33]

And so the debate gradually moved to a new stage—not just over the feasibility of government without hereditary rule, but over the forms of the new republican governments. Could the American states remain "simple Republics" like the congresses and conventions of 1774–76, or did "the great distinction of persons, and difference in their estates or property" require some further adaptation of "mixed government"? If governors and upper houses were to be revived, could domestic tranquillity be maintained? Need those institutions be considered the "dregs of Monarchical and Aristocratical tyranny," or could they also represent the people and so be compatible with republicanism? Then, too, there was the question whether virtue, with its component of deference, would be maintained under republican government—of what effect the Revolution would actually have on the social and political order.[34]

As the fuller democratic meaning of republicanism was worked out in the 1780's and 1790's, expanding the effects of the Revolution, some of the old revolutionaries were caught unaware and reflected on their commitment of 1776 with mixed feelings. At that earlier time, however, the option for republicanism was logical, even obvious given their experiences of the previous decade. The alternative of limited monarchy had proven illusory: if the "best of Kings" could become "the royal brute of Britain," making "havoc of mankind," no monarchy could be adequately restrained. The crown must be "demolished and scattered among the people," whose right it was.[35] Meanwhile republicanism, once considered utopian, assumed practicality. Recent American experience suggested that it alone could provide the freedom, peace, and security that all men sought of government.

Notes

[1] Gadsden, "To the Gentlemen Electors of the Parish of St. Paul, Stono," Feb. 5, 1763, in Richard Walsh, ed., *The Writings of Christopher Gadsden, 1746–1805* (Columbia, S. C., University of South Carolina Press, 1966), p. 48; *New York Journal*, Sept. 1, 1774; resolutions of the Newport Sons of Liberty, Apr. 2, 1766, Rhode Island Historical Society Manuscripts XII, f. 66, Rhode Island Historical Society, Providence, R.I.; Portsmouth, N.H., Sons of Liberty to Providence Sons, Portsmouth, Apr. 10, 1766, Belknap papers, 61.c.122, Massachusetts Historical Society, Boston.

This paper constitutes a further development of the argument presented in the concluding chapter of Pauline Maier's *From Resistance to Revolution: Colonial Radicals and the Development of American Opposition to Britain, 1765–1776* (New York, Alfred A. Knopf, 1972).

[2] Cecelia M. Kenyon, "Republicanism and Radicalism in the American Revolution: An Old-Fashioned Interpretation," *William and Mary Quarterly*, 3d ser., 19(1962):168; R. R. Palmer, *The Age of the Democratic Revolution*, vol. 1 (Princeton, Princeton University Press, 1959).

[3] W. Paul Adams, "Republicanism in Political Rhetoric Before 1776," *Political Science Quarterly*, 85(1970):397–421.

[4] Kenyon, "Republicanism and Radicalism," p. 165.

[5] Paine, "Dissertations on Government," and also "The Rights of Man," in Philip S. Foner, ed., *The Complete Writings of Thomas Paine* (New York, The Citadel Press, 1969), vol. 2, p. 372–373, and vol. 1, p. 369.

[6] See John Locke, *The Second Treatise of Government*, Thomas P. Peardon, ed. (New York, Liberal Arts Press, 1952), para. 131: "the power of the society, or legislative constituted by them, can never be supposed to extend farther than the common good. . . ." See also John Trenchard and Thomas Gordon, *Cato's Letters* (6th ed., London, Printed for J. Walthoe . . ., 1755), vol. 1, p. 179–180: "Government executed for the Good of All, and with the Consent of All, is Liberty. . . ."

[7] See Adams, "Republicanism in Political Rhetoric," p. 402 n. and 403 for Molesworth quotation; Gerald Stourzh, *Alexander Hamilton and the Idea of Republican Government* (Stanford, Stanford University Press, 1970), p. 45–46.

[8] Trenchard and Gordon, *Cato's Letters*, vol. 3, p. 159–160, 162–163, and quotation by them in Staughton Lynd, *Intellectual Origins of American Radicalism* (New York, Vintage, 1969), p. 22. Caroline Robbins, *The Eighteenth-Century Commonwealthman* (Cambridge, Mass., Harvard University Press, 1961).

[9] *Constitutional Courant* in *Publications of the Colonial Society of Massachusetts*, vol. 11, p. 426 (Its *Transactions*, 1906–7); Connecticut Sons of Liberty to Portsmouth, N.H., Sons of Liberty, Norwich, Conn., Mar. 3, 1766, Belknap papers, 61.c.118.

[10] *New York Journal*, Oct. 1, 1767; Maier, *From Resistance to Revolution*, p. 174–175, 200–213, 237–241.

[11] Palfrey to Wilkes, Boston, Oct. 23–30, 1770, *Publications of the Colonial Society of Massachusetts*, vol. 24, p. 421 (Its *Transactions*, 1937–42); *Massachusetts Spy*, Apr. 8, 1773; speech of Sept. 27 in *New London* (Conn.) *Gazette*, Dec. 22, 1775; "Salus Populi" (1776) in Peter Force, ed., *American Archives*, 4th ser. (Washington, M. St. Clair Clarke and Peter Force, 1837–46), vol. 5, p. 182. See also Richard Parker to Richard Henry Lee, Apr. 27, 1776, Lee family papers, University of Virginia Library, Charlottesville, available in Paul P. Hoffman, ed., "Lee Family Papers, 1742–1795," University of Virginia microfilm (Charlottesville, 1966), roll II.

[12] Article from the *London Public Ledger* in *New London Gazette*, Oct. 7, 1774.

[13] Arthur Lee to Samuel Adams, Dec. 10, 1775, Samuel Adams papers, New York Public Library, New York; "Monitor," *New York Journal*, Jan. 25, 1776; "A Republican," *Massachusetts Spy*, Apr. 8, 1773. See also "Salus Populi" in Force, ed., *American Archives*, 4th ser., vol. 5, p. 181: "Kings and nobles are artificial beings, for whose emolument civil society was never intended; . . . I will boldly affirm that nine-tenths of all the publick calamities which ever befell mankind, were brought on by their means."

[14] Article from *Pennsylvania Packet* in *Providence Gazette*, Dec. 17, 1774; Princeton oration in *New London Gazette*, Dec. 22, 1775; "A Republican," *Massachusetts Spy*, Apr. 8, 1773; article from *St. James Chronicle* in *Boston Gazette*, Sept. 18, 1775.

[15] *Boston Gazette*, Sept. 18, 1775; article from *London Public Ledger* in *New London Gazette*, Oct. 7, 1774, and from *London Chronicle* in *Pennsylvania Journal*, Apr. 13, 1774; Paine, "Common Sense," in Foner, ed., *Paine Writings*, vol. 1, p. 14.

[16] John Trenchard, *An History of Standing Armies in England....* (London, 1739), p. 1. Paine, "Common Sense," in Foner, ed., *Paine Writings*, vol. 1, p. 7, 9. Stiles to Catharine Macaulay, Dec. 6, 1773, Ezra Stiles papers, Beinecke Library, Yale University, New Haven, Conn.

[17] George P. Anderson, "Pascal Paoli, An Inspiration to the Sons of Liberty," *Publications of the Colonial Society of Massachusetts*, vol. 26, p. 184 (Its *Transactions*, 1924–26); Catharine Macaulay, *Loose Remarks on Certain Positions to be Found in Mr. Hobbes's Philosophical Rudiments of Government and Society. With a Short Sketch of a Democratical Form of Government in a Letter to Signior Paoli ... With Two Letters, one from an American Gentleman...* (2d ed., London, Printed for W. Johnston ..., 1769); Stiles to Macaulay, Dec. 6, 1773, Stiles papers.

[18] Stiles to Macaulay, Dec. 6, 1773, Stiles papers; Hooper to James Iredell, Apr. 26, 1774, *Colonial Records of North Carolina*, vol. 9 (Raleigh, 1890), p. 985; Hollis to Josiah Quincy, Jr., Mar. 2, 1775, Josiah Quincy, Jr., papers, f. 97, Massachusetts Historical Society, Boston. Hooper emphasized the extent of England's "dominion" rather than monarchy as the cause of her downfall.

[19] "A Freeman" to Pennsylvania Assembly, July 21, 1774, Force, ed., *American Archives*, 4th ser., vol. 1, p. 607; Adams, "Republicanism in Political Rhetoric," p. 414–415, including quotation from "Civis," *Pennsylvania Ledger*, Apr. 6, 1776; "A Native" (1776), in Force, ed., *American Archives*, 4th ser., vol. 6, p. 751–752.

[20] Warren, in Force, ed., *American Archives*, 4th ser., vol. 2, p. 43; "Journal of Josiah Quincy, Jun., During his Voyage and Residence in England from September 28th, 1774, to March 3d, 1775," *Proceedings of the Massachusetts Historical Society*, vol. 50 (1916–17), p. 469; Ld. Edmond Fitzmaurice, *Charles William Ferdinand, Duke of Brunswick; an Historical Study, 1735–1806* (London, Longmans, Green, & Co., 1901), esp. p. 14–16.

[21] Warren to Adams, Cambridge, May 14, 1775, in Richard Frothingham, *Life and Times of Joseph Warren* (Boston, Little, Brown & Co., 1865), p. 483; John Adams to Archibald Bullock, July 1, 1776, in Charles Francis Adams, ed., *The Works of John Adams* (Boston, Little, Brown & Co., 1850–56), vol. 9, p. 414.

[22] Jack P. Greene, "The Role of the Lower Houses of Assembly in Eighteenth-Century Politics," in Greene, ed., *The Reinterpretation of the American Revolution* (New York, Harper & Row, 1968), passim and p. 95; also Greene, *The Quest for Power: The Lower Houses of Assembly in the Southern Royal Colonies, 1689–1776* (Chapel Hill, University of North Carolina Press, 1963). J. H. Pole, *The Seventeenth Century: The Sources of Legislative Power* (Charlottesville, University of Virginia Press, 1969), p. 69.

[23] Bernard Bailyn, *The Origins of American Politics* (New York, Vintage, 1968), p. 59–63, 66–70; Greene, *Reinterpretation of the American Revolution*, p. 22.

[24] See Maier, *Resistance to Revolution*, p. 35–36, 87–89, 116.

[25] Virginia Associations of May 18, 1769, and June 22, 1770, in Julian Boyd, ed., *The Papers of Thomas Jefferson*, vol. 1 (Princeton, Princeton University Press, 1950), p. 27–31, 43–48; Maryland Association of June 22, 1769, in *Maryland Historical Magazine*, 3(1908):144–149; "Continental Association," in J. R. Pole, ed., *The Revolution in America, 1754–1788* (Stanford, Stanford University Press, 1970), p. 24–29.

[26] William Henry Drayton, *The Letters of Freeman* ... (London, 1771), p. 119; Dunmore to Lord Dartmouth, Williamsburg, Dec. 24, 1774, in Richard B. Harwell, ed., *Proceedings of the County Committees, 1774–1776: The Committees of Safety of Westmoreland and Fincastle* (Richmond, Virginia State Library, 1956), p. 19; New York Congress resolves, in Force, ed., *American Archives*, 4th ser., vol. 4, p. 435; letter to *Connecticut Gazette* reprinted in *New London Gazette*, Oct. 21, 1774.

[27] *Newport Mercury*, Apr. 7, 1766; Albany "constitution," in *The American Historian*, vol. 1 (Schenectady, 1876), p. 145–146; Maier, *Resistance to Revolution*, p. 96–100.

[28] Dickinson, "Letters from a Farmer in Pennsylvania," in Forrest McDonald, ed., *Empire and Nation* (Englewood Cliffs, N.J., Prentice-Hall, 1962), p. 15–20; Mason to Richard Henry Lee, June 7, 1770, in Kate Mason Rowland, *The Life of George Mason* (New York, G. P. Putnam's Sons, 1892), vol. 1, p. 144; Richard D. Brown, *Revolutionary Politics in Massachusetts* (Cambridge, Harvard University Press, 1970), p. 212–220; Frederick Freeman, *The History of Cape Cod* (Boston, Rand & Avery, 1860), vol. 1, p. 430–432; Maier, *Resistance to Revolution*, p. 120–131, 274–287.

[29] Mercy Warren, *History of the Rise, Progress, and Termination of the American Revolution*, vol. 1 (Boston, Printed by Manning & Loring, for E. Larkin, 1805), p. 153. For a series of similar reactions see Gordon Wood, *The Creation of the American Republic, 1776–1789* (Chapel Hill, University of North Carolina Press, 1969), p. 102–103.

[30] *Ibid.*, p. 102–103, 77; Warren, *History*, vol. 1, p. 151; Pocock, "Virtue and Commerce in the Eighteenth Century," *Journal of Interdisciplinary History*, 3(summer 1972): 124; John to Abigail Adams, May 17, 1776, in L. H. Butterfield, ed., *Adams Family Correspondence*, vol. 1 (New York, Atheneum, 1965), p. 411. Paine, "Common Sense," in Foner, ed., *Paine Writings*, vol. 1, p. 27.

[31] "Common Sense," in Foner, ed., *Paine Writings*, vol. 1, p. 27.

[32] "Salus Populi," in Force, ed., *American Archives*, 4th ser., vol. 5, p. 180; Stourzh, *Alexander Hamilton*, p. 49, and also 48.

[33] "Salus Populi," in Force, ed., *American Archives*, 4th ser., vol. 5, p. 180–181; "The Interest of America" (1776), *ibid.*, vol. 6, p. 841–842.

[34] "On the Present State of Affairs in America" by "A Farmer," Philadelphia, Nov. 5, 1776, and resolutions of Chesterfield, N.Y., Committee, Dec. 12, 1776, in Force, ed., *American Archives*, 5th ser., vol. 3 (Washington, 1853), p. 518 and 1226. See also Wood, *Creation of the American Republic*; and Pauline Maier, "The Charles-

ton Mob and the Evolution of Popular Politics in Revolutionary South Carolina, 1765–1784," *Perspectives in American History*, vol. 4 (1970): 186–196.

35 Paine, "Common Sense," in Foner, ed., *Paine Writings*, vol. 1, p. 29.

Jack P. Greene holds a B.A. degree from the University of North Carolina, an M.A. from Indiana University, and a Ph.D. from Duke University. He has taught at Michigan State University, Western Reserve University, and the University of Michigan. In 1966 he was appointed to his present position as professor of history at The Johns Hopkins University. Professor Greene is a member of the advisory committee of the Library of Congress American Revolution Bicentennial program.

Among Professor Greene's numerous historical studies are The Quest for Power: The Lower Houses of Assembly in the Southern Royal Colonies, 1689–1776 *(1963),* The Diary of Colonel Landon Carter of Sabine Hall, 1752–1778 *(1965),* Settlements to Society, 1584–1763 *(1966),* Colonies to Nation, 1763–1789 *(1967),* The Reappraisal of the American Revolution in Recent Historical Literature *(1967),* The Ambiguity of the American Revolution *(1968), and* The Reinterpretation of the American Revolution, 1763–1789 *(1968). He has also served as visiting editor of the* William and Mary Quarterly.

MANY OF US know and admire the contributions of Jack Greene to our knowledge of the legislative process in colonial America and to a wide variety of other subjects to which he has devoted his attention and over which he has an encyclopedic command. His perceptive *Reinterpretation of the American Revolution* has performed a miraculous job of distillation and is guaranteed a long life far beyond the termination of the Bicentennial celebration.

The Preconditions for American Republicanism: A Comment

JACK P. GREENE

IN HER THOUGHTFUL ANALYSIS of the transformation in the colonists' attitudes toward republicanism between 1765 and 1775, Professor Maier has traced the process by and outlined the conditions under which the colonists passed from a deep and passionate rejection to a profound and avid embrace of republicanism as the political philosophy and the form of government most appropriate for and most congenial to the genius of the American people.[1] She has described—and I think intends to account for—this transformation in terms of two interrelated and well-known developments during the late 1760's and the early 1770's: the conjoint disillusion of the colonists with monarchy as a result of their growing hostility to George III and the colonists' successful experimentation with republicanism through "the associations formed to regularize colonial resistance to British legislation." In her handling of this second point, Professor Maier goes well beyond any previous analyst in demonstrating the "protorepublican" character of the associations and committees and in explaining how their successful functioning seemed to serve as a practical demonstration of the viability of republican institutions in a British-American setting. Much more fully than any previous writer, she also calls our attention to a considerable number of instances in which colonial disillusionment with George III was accompanied by the questioning of the appropriateness and/or legitimacy of monarchy as an institution. On the basis of the evidence she presents both in her paper and in her recent book, the extent of that questioning before Lexington and Concord remains, I think, an unresolved question. At the very least, however, she has made it clear that the explicit attack on monarchy in the colonies, however confined, began five years earlier than we have traditionally believed.

As an explanation for the question of why the Americans embraced republicanism in the mid-1770's, however, I find Professor Maier's paper incomplete, incomplete in that she fails to put the transformation she describes in its broadest context. She has indeed gone a long way toward describing how some of the more important deterrents which originally prevented Americans from considering republicanism were removed, but she has not explicitly addressed herself to the question of why that transformation occurred so extraordinarily easily. The answer, I submit, is to be found not only in the accumulated experience with republican associations and the simultaneous growth of an aversion to monarchy and an attachment to republicanism but also, and even more importantly, in the simple fact that, once the colonists had opted for independence, there simply was no other available alternative. The suggestion by a man with radical proclivities as strong as those of Joseph Warren that Karl Wilhelm Ferdinand become an American monarch is indeed a striking indication of the extreme difficulties Americans had in rejecting monarchy and the other components of the British Constitution, of the great emotional difficulties they had in letting go of their ancient connection with Britain and the symbols of that connection, but it scarcely can be taken as evidence that monarchy was a viable alternative for an independent America.

Nor is it by any means clear that Whig Americans universally embraced republicanism with the unquestioning enthusiasm that Professor Maier, following Gordon Wood's recent argument,[2] has suggested. During the mid-1770's some political leaders (and followers) did indeed seize upon republicanism as a panacea which would bring about "a widespread reformation of American politics and society." That such an attitude was dominant in American political thought, that it was representative of the central and most pervasive impulses within the spirit of 1776, has not, however, been convincingly demonstrated. Whatever degree of self-sacrifice and devotion to the public good had been displayed by the colonists during the crisis of 1774–76, there were nagging and widespread doubts, doubts confirmed by long experience, that human nature, though, as one Whig remarked, perhaps in some ways "better situated,"[3] was any different in America than it was in Britain and that the American people had the virtue requisite for the successful operation of a republic. Hence, the intense and widespread demonstration of concern among the State constitution-makers, even in Pennsylvania, to devise institutional contrivances that might make it possible for imperfect and unvirtuous men, rulers and ruled alike, to live together in a republic.

Nor could the successful functioning of the "republican" associations really remove these doubts. As Whig theorists and others acquainted with the history of their parent state in the mid-17th century must have known, similar associations had sprung up in England and Scotland during the opening stages of the English Revolution and enjoyed an equal degree of success and celebration.[4] But they had scarcely been a harbinger of the success of the Commonwealth.

But the important point, again, is that whatever fears or hopes American Whigs had about the viability of republicanism in 1776, they had no other choice. There could be, and were, serious disagreements over precisely how popular the republican governments they established might be, but independence and republicanism were understood to be closely associated by 1776 precisely because independence necessarily meant, and was widely understood by people of all political persuasions to mean, republicanism.

To understand why the range of alternatives open to Whig leaders was so restricted requires not merely an analysis of the changing orientation of American political thought in the decade before 1776 but a consideration of the underlying social and political circumstances within American life that rendered monarchy an inappropriate political solution for an independent America and constituted the essential preconditions—and hence must be a necessary part of any explanation—for the American conversion and adoption of republicanism in the mid-1770's.

The broad outlines of what such a consideration would reveal are, I think, fairly clear. For as many British observers and virtually all American Tories so thoroughly understood, once the imperial superstructure had been removed, the ingredients for a successful monarchy were entirely missing from the American scene. As William Knox, undersecretary for the colonies with experience as a royal officeholder in Georgia, pointed out in trying to explain why the American Revolution had occurred, the very conditions of both private and public life in America had militated against the development of "all [of those] ideas of subordination and dependence" that were thought to be requisite for the successful functioning of monarchy. The failure to establish a proper religious hierarchy, the wide distribution of property, and the absence of a middle or aristocratic estate had all served, Knox and many others thought, to destroy whatever feelings "of subordination that property, ancestry or dignity of station ... naturally excited" among Britons in the home islands. Moreover, the political systems of the colonies were, and had always been, only marginally compatible with monarchy. Nor was it merely the New England colonies, two of which were "republics pure and simple," that were "tinctured with republicanism"; even in the royal colonies, Knox contended, "the Democracy had the leading influence and the general tendency" was to republicanism, a general tendency that "increased with their wealth, & in a little time, if their prosperity had continued must," even without the Revolution, "have swallowed up the monarchic powers." This widespread, to use Knox's words again, "adoption of the commonwealth-mode" was,[5] I think, largely what J. R. Pole had in mind in the observation quoted by Professor Maier that "the American Colonies developed the characteristics of what would later be known as a republican form of government many years before they were to claim to be republican in principle."

Given these powerful underlying tendencies toward republicanism and such enormously favorable conditions for its development as well as the additional practical experience with republicanism gained by the colonists during the prerevolutionary controversy, the single most striking feature of the American conversion to republicanism was not that it occurred so fast but that it took so long. The reasons for this slowness, the central deterrents to the colonists' acceptance of republicanism, are to be found partly in the deep ideological aversion to republicanism within Anglo-American political culture, an aversion that has been discussed by Professor Maier and has been delineated even more fully by W. Paul Adams in a recent article.[6] A related and more important deterrent, which Professor Maier alludes to only briefly at the very beginning of her paper, was the pervasive affection for and loyalty to Britain within the colonies. This affection and loyalty derived not only from the fact that the colonists were predominantly British in origin, not merely from the colonists' habitual and deep dependence upon Britain for political and cultural authority, for authoritative institutions and symbols of legitimacy, and not simply from the pride and self-esteem they derived from having a share, if often largely only peripheral and even vicarious, in the internal civil and religious achievements of Great Britain following the Glorious Revolution and the economic and military accomplishments represented by the enormous expansion of foreign trade and the overwhelming victory over the French and Spanish in the Seven Years' War. The affection derived as well from the colonists' profound dependence upon Britain for evaluative standards and models of behavior, standards and models of what America and Americans ultimately ought to and hoped to become. Given the longstanding—and, I suspect, increasing—anxiety within America about the colonists' demonstrated moral deficiencies, it was an open question as to whether or not America could survive as a free society without those standards—and the connection which supplied and reinforced them.[7] For all of these reasons, then, the colonists were so deeply dependent upon Britain, so strongly committed to the central components of British political culture that any doctrine such as republicanism that was thought to be antithetical to the fundamental postulates of British social and political life was illegitimate and therefore outside the limits of acceptable political discourse within the colonies. As the earlier work of Edmund S. Morgan, Bernard Bailyn, Professor Maier, and several others has shown so clearly and forcefully, a significant erosion of British moral authority and a considerable deflation of British power was required—that is, a major desacralization of the existing moral order which bound the colonies so tightly to Britain had to occur— before Britain's powerful normative resources in the colonies could be sufficiently dissipated to permit the lapse of the repressions that had long prevented the colonists from taking a more positive attitude toward hitherto illegitimate ideas such as independence and republicanism, before republicanism could become in fact an idea with some competitive power with monarchy.[8]

To produce a comprehensive explanation for the emergence of republicanism in America in the mid-1770's, we will have to move beyond the analysis of its intellectual aspects, fascinating as they may be, and immediate political origins, important as they may be, to an exploration of the social conditions that facilitated and the emotional conditions that deterred its acceptance. For together these social and emotional conditions had a profound and, in Professor Maier's paper as well as in the symposium as a whole, an insufficiently appreciated bearing upon the development of a revolutionary mentality—the general theme of this volume.

Notes

[1] These comments, necessarily brief because of my failure, for many reasons beyond Professor Maier's control, to receive a copy of her paper until just prior to the symposium, appear here as they were delivered orally with only a few minor verbal changes.

[2] In *The Creation of the American Republic, 1776–1787* (Chapel Hill, University of North Carolina Press, 1969), 653 p.

[3] The quotation is from an essay by Landon Carter in the Williamsburg *Virginia Gazette* (Rind), Apr. 21, 1770.

[4] See, especially, Alan Milner Everitt, *The County Committee of Kent in the Civil War* (Leicester, Eng., University College of Leicester, 1957), 54 p.

[5] The Knox quotations are from his "Considerations on the great Question, what is to be done with America? Part First," [1778–79], Gower Papers, PRO 30/29/3/6, ff. 556–573, Public Record Office, London. See also Knox's opening essay in *Extra Official State Papers* (London, 1789), vol. 2, p. 20–22.

[6] "Republicanism in Political Rhetoric Before 1776," *Political Science Quarterly*, 85 (Sept. 1970):397–421.

[7] See Jack P. Greene, "Search for Identity: An Interpretation of Selected Patterns of Social Response in Eighteenth-Century America," *Journal of Social History*, 3 (Spring 1970):189–220.

[8] For an elaboration of this argument, see Jack P. Greene, "An Uneasy Connection: An Analysis of the Preconditions of the American Revolution," in Stephen G. Kurtz and James H. Hutson, eds., *Essays on the American Revolution* (Chapel Hill, University of North Carolina Press, forthcoming).

Mary Beth Norton received her B.A. degree from the University of Michigan and her M.A. and Ph.D. degrees from Harvard University, where she was a Woodrow Wilson Fellow and a Harvard Prize Fellow. The Society of American Historians awarded her its 1969 Allan Nevins Prize for the outstanding doctoral dissertation in American history. Professor Norton has taught at the University of Connecticut at Storrs and, since 1971, at Cornell University. She is the author of The British-Americans: The Loyalist Exiles in England, 1774–1789 *(1972).*

ONE HUNDRED TWENTY-FIVE YEARS AGO, when Lorenzo Sabine had the courage to publish his biographical sketches of loyalists of the American Revolution, he suffered ostracism for his presumption. The loyalists remained "untouchables" and "unmentionables," and the Tory was traditionally assailed as one "whose head is in England, whose body is in America, and whose neck should be stretched." We have traveled a long road since then, and recent writers have treated the first American civil war for what it was, a difference between Englishmen, both sides conscientious in their convictions. Of the recent writers on the loyalists, Mary Beth Norton has chosen to study them as exiles in England. I have not had the advantage of reading her work, which was awarded a Nevins Prize and is considered a topnotch study. I am sure that her paper will whet our appetite for the book itself, which bears the title *The British-Americans, 1774–1788.*

The Loyalist Critique
of the Revolution

MARY BETH NORTON

THE TERM "AMERICAN TORY" tends to conjure up a standard image in the minds of modern Americans who have not studied the revolutionary period in detail. That image can be quickly sketched. The Tories were wealthy colonial aristocrats—merchants, landowners, and officeholders—who, for selfish, even venal motives, opposed the fight for independence. They were ultraconservatives who resisted change of any sort. Most likely, they were members of the Church of England. Many of them had probably been born in the British Isles. Their status, their religion, and their political philosophy therefore combined to render them unsympathetic to the Americans' struggle against British oppression. Perhaps we should not today condemn them as traitors, but on the other hand their continuing loyalty to the empire stands as incontrovertible evidence of their opposition to the best interests of their country.

The revolutionaries, by contrast, are usually seen as dissenters in religion, as virtuous lower and middle class colonists, as men who recognized that America had to free herself from British tyranny and who accordingly risked their lives for an ideal of human liberty. The loyalists, in other words, are believed to have been aberrations, and so they are viewed as a small, self-interested minority. Among citizens of the United States today, it is widely and uncritically assumed that any truly patriotic American would have supported the Revolution.

Historians are forever congratulating themselves on their ability to escape the confines of such popular fictions as the one just outlined. And, with respect to the Tories, they have succeeded in part. It is now generally accepted that most loyalists were rather ordinary people: there were "aristocrats" among them, but the vast majority were small farmers, shopkeepers, laborers, and the like. By no means were they all Anglicans, nor were they necessarily British-born. In demographic terms, they were not very different from their revolutionary compatriots.[1] But the demythologizing has not yet gone far enough. Historians still tend to view the loyalists as aberrations that have to be explained away, as persons who somehow stand outside the "normal" trend of American development. The very term that is most commonly used to designate them contributes to this opinion: where, after all, does a "Tory" fit into what we now regard as an overwhelmingly whiggish 18th-century America?

To those who think I am being too harsh on contemporary historians, I would address the following questions: Why is it that we always ask what caused *this* man to be a loyalist but rarely ask what caused *that* man to be a revolutionary? Why is it that almost every recent study of the loyalists has had their motivations as one of its major concerns? And, most importantly, why is it that studies of the Revolution, or textbook accounts of it, devote very little space to considering the opposition to the movement for independence? One has only to contrast the historical treatment of the Tories, the losers in the first American civil war, with the usual treatment accorded men who chose the losing side in the second, a hundred years later, to see the point. Moreover, it seems instructive to note that even if historians are willing to grant the loyalists the courage of their convictions, they seem incapable of regarding a man like Thomas Hutchinson as an American patriot in the same sense that Thomas Jefferson and John Adams are commonly interpreted as American patriots.

The purpose of this paper, then, is twofold: first, to take some tentative steps toward removing the implicit bias that has shaped our view of the loyalists, and second, to demonstrate that, once that bias is removed, a number of intriguing observations emerge from previously obscure sources. The vehicle for achieving this end will be a reinterpretation of loyalist commentaries on the issues of the Revolution.

1

The first problem that must be dealt with is the use of the word "Tory" to describe colonists who remained loyal to Great Britain. It takes but a brief glance at works on the subject of English political ideology in the 17th and 18th centuries to discover that American Tories were not Tories at all in the traditional English sense of that term. They were certainly not Jacobites who hoped to perpetuate the Stuart line of British monarchs. They did not oppose the constitutional settlement of 1688. Some indeed were concerned with maintaining a close relationship between church and state, but they were little interested in the political issues that moved English Tories in the 18th century.[2]

Why, then, have these Americans been called Tories? One plausible answer is that the revolutionaries dubbed them as such to take advantage of the pejorative connotation of that word in the whiggish colonies. Americans gloried in the name of Whig and venerated the Glorious Revolution. What better means to discredit opponents of a particular position than to charge them with being Tories? Another possible explanation is that "Tory" was utilized only as a synonym for "conservative." Therefore, it can be contended, there need be no ideological connection between English and American Toryism for the term to be accurately applicable to colonial circumstances. The point is perhaps well taken, but if conservative is defined as consistently opposing change, then that word does not describe the loyalists either.

A further and even more telling response is to argue that the loyalists are called Tories because that was what they termed themselves. It can, for example, be pointed out that in 1797 the exiled Maryland clergyman Jonathan Boucher wrote that "the American Revolution was clearly a struggle for preeminence between Whigs and Tories." His characterization was not merely one of hindsight, for in 1774 a young attorney, Daniel Leonard, had utilized the same terms to discuss the party conflict he perceived in prerevolutionary Massachusetts. And yet there was a difficulty inherent in the party designations, and Leonard was well aware of it. He explained, "The terms whig and tory have been adopted according to the arbitrary use of them in this province, but they rather ought to be reversed; an American tory is a supporter of our excellent constitution, and an American whig a subverter of it."[3]

Here indeed is the central paradox of what has been called Toryism in the colonial context. The "American Tory" was in fact a Whig par excellence: he was a vehement supporter of the settlement resulting from the Glorious Revolution and a fervent admirer of the British Constitution.[4] He was in the mainstream of 18th-century English whiggery: it was the American revolutionaries who, in the imperial world, were the aberrations. As has recently been made clear by a number of works, the thought of colonial radicals was largely derived from a singular, unorthodox branch of Whig ideology, one that had little credence among most Englishmen. Moreover, the Americans had changed and adapted that strain of thinking to fit their rather peculiar circumstances, with the result that by the time of the Revolution it bore an increasingly tenuous relationship to its origins.[5]

In sum, instead of characterizing the American Revolution as a struggle between Whigs and Tories, I would argue that in ideological terms it should be seen as a contest between different varieties of Whigs, Whigs whose respective world views brought some of them to become revolutionaries and others to become loyalists—not Tories, for that word shall henceforth disappear from my vocabulary. It has been recognized for several years that some loyalists at least can be termed Whigs;[6] I would simply extend that designation to enclose the ranks of almost all of them.

One immediate indication of the loyalists' political sympathies is the fact that their authors cited the same standard Whig authorities as did revolutionary writers. Copious references to Locke, Hume, Montesquieu, Grotius, and Vattel line the pages of works by Joseph Galloway and other loyal essayists.[7] It might, of course, be argued that these citations were simply window dressing designed to fool unwary colonists into believing that they were reading Whig theory when in fact they were not, but a close look at loyalist writings shows that these men did indeed view society and government through a whiggish lens.

The loyalists, with the exception of one man who will be considered shortly, unhesitatingly accepted the Lockean explanation for the origins of government. In 1783 Galloway wrote, "Civil society is a political system, formed by the union of individuals, who, putting their several powers under one sovereign direction for their better security, agree to yield obedience to it." Other loyalists like Isaac Hunt and Jacob Duché, both of whom were Philadelphians, agreed that "true government can have no other foundation than COMMON CONSENT." Furthermore, added Daniel Batwell, another Pennsylvanian, the only legitimate government was one that respected "the natural rights of mankind."[8] Even those loyalists who are generally regarded as being more conservative than the ones just cited expressed a concern for the preservation of individual liberty within the social structure. In nearly identical phraseology, the New York clergymen Samuel Seabury and Charles Inglis declared that they believed that Americans—indeed, all men—had "a right to as much freedom as is consistent with the security of civil society." That this formula was not simply a "code phrase" for acquiescence in the wishes of the government is shown by the fact that the revolutionaries also used the same sort of definition for civil liberty.[9]

Moreover, the loyalists did not believe that the government could do no wrong. "A right to do what is reasonable, implies not a right to do what is unreasonable," wrote Thomas Bradbury Chandler, an Anglican clergyman, in 1774. "Every society has a right to make a moderate use of its power over its own members, but not to abuse it." In this Chandler was simply following the standard argument, derived from Locke, that a government, however supreme its powers, could not exercise its authority arbitrarily.[10] The loyalists therefore joined the revolutionaries in admitting that an oppressive use of political power gave the injured populace a right to seek redress of its grievances. Peter Van Schaack, a New York attorney, asserted in 1776 that there could be no question "about the lawfulness of resistance, in cases of gross and palpable infractions on the part of the governing power." He was in perfect agreement with that supposed arch-conservative, Thomas Hutchinson, who had commented casually a year earlier, "Not that I ever supposed the people of any Govt are under such moral obligations to any System as that when the general safety requires it they are not at liberty to depart from it."[11] One can also cite Galloway's similar statement: "Should a State arbitrarily deprive its members of their just rights, and refuse to restore them, after it has been repeatedly, and respectfully required so to do, then their duties and obedience to the state cease." It must be conceded that Galloway added three words to the end of this line, so that it reads, "then their duties and obedience to the state cease, but not before," but that does not change the theoretical import of his declaration, only its specific interpretation.[12]

As noted earlier, there was one exception to this general whiggish rule, and that was Jonathan Boucher, the Anglican cleric who openly rejected Lockean thought. Boucher ridiculed the idea of "some imaginary compact" formed by primitive men "in a rude and imperfect state of society." He turned instead to the work of Filmer for an explanation of the origins of government, concluding that "the first father was the first king ... it was thus that all government originated," so monarchy was "it's most ancient form." There was no right of resistance, Boucher asserted; "all government ... is, in it's nature, absolute and irresistible." Consequently, every subject owed obedience to his *"governors, teachers, spiritual pastors, and masters."*[13]

But even Boucher qualified his sentiments on occasion. In his 1797 introduction to the book of sermons published as *A View of the Causes and Consequences of the American Revolution*, Boucher admitted that, however undesirable they were, revolutions might sometimes be "if not necessary, yet useful in States, by bringing forward some improvements in Government." He also consistently rejected the contention that he advocated *"unlimited obedience"* to "despotic" states. Rather, Boucher insisted, he thought only *"passive obedience"* was necessary. This latter he defined as a willingness "patiently to submit to the penalties annexed to disobedience, where that which is commanded by man is forbidden by God."[14] Furthermore, Boucher denied only the right to resist a *lawful* government, thus leaving open the question of whether it might be possible to resist an *unlawful* one. And, when he set out to define liberty, to whom did he look but the same Locke whose ideas on the social compact he so resoundingly criticized. Freedom could be obtained only through law, Boucher argued in a Lockean vein; the goal of "all well-framed Constitutions" was "to place man, as it were, out of the reach of his own power, and also out of the power of others as weak as himself, by placing him under the power of law."[15]

The point here is not that Boucher was a Lockean in spite of himself; rather, it appears that even he, the most conservative, or Tory-like, if you will, of all the loyalists, was influenced by some of the themes of 18th-century whiggery. And most of those Americans who joined him in opposing the Revolution were far more deeply affected by Lockean modes of thought than he was.

Turning from theoretical issues to specific colonial circumstances, it is important to realize that, in addition to being ideological Whigs, the loyalists felt a deep and abiding love for America. Most of them accordingly had a large measure of sympathy for colonial protests against British policies. Their comments on American grievances indicate that they were neither unthinking tools of the British ministry nor rigid conservatives who resisted all change within the empire. To the contrary, many loyalists fully recognized the necessity of a readjustment in the relationship of the colonies and the mother country.

Thomas Bradbury Chandler, for example, declared in 1775 that Americans did not "enjoy all the privileges of Englishmen, while we give no kind of consent to the laws that govern us," and, he concluded, "it is time that we were exempted, in a regular way, from parliamentary taxation, on some generous and equitable plan." Even such a staunchly conservative man as Jonathan Boucher supported the American protests against the Stamp and Townshend Acts and did not retreat from a whiggish stance until 1772–73.[16]

Other loyalists went much farther than Chandler or Boucher. William Smith, for one, concluded in June 1776 that "the present Animosities are imputable to the Pride & Avarice of Great Britain, in assuming an Authority, inconsistant with the Compact by which the Empire have been so long prosperously united." He particularly criticized the "new and awful Idea of the Constitution" inherent in the Stamp Act and the "pestilent Influence" of the Declaratory Act. Smith thought the Americans' resistance to the Tea Act entirely justifiable and the British reaction to that resistance (that is, the Intolerable Acts) "utterly unjustifiable." He accordingly accused Britain of "commencing an unnecessary War to maintain an illiberal Dominion."[17] In much the same vein were the comments of Smith's fellow New Yorker Peter Van Schaack, who described the Intolerable Acts as "truly alarming" and told a friend that if it was not the colonists' "*right*" to be exempt from parliamentary taxation, then "they do not enjoy the privileges of British subjects." As early as February 1774 he wrote, "The absurdity of uniting the idea of a right in the Americans to the liberties of Englishmen, with that of a subordination to the British Parliament, is every day growing more evident."[18]

Galloway accurately expressed the loyalists' viewpoint in 1775. Writing of the First Continental Congress, he declared, "I do not differ from them in opinion, that America has grievances to complain of; but I differ from them in the mode of *obtaining redress*." As Galloway saw it, the colonies had three alternatives: submit to Parliament, resist and be conquered by Britain's superior forces, or "seek for redress in an *union* with the Mother State." The last was his choice, and it was the choice of many of his fellow loyalists as well. They recognized, in Boucher's words, that "our Constitution, admirable as it is, is not, it wou'd seem, wholly adapted to all the Purposes of Government in large Adjuncts of the Empire neither foreseen, nor provided for, when this Constitution was formed."[19] The obvious solution to the colonies' problems, therefore, was to obtain "a general *American Constitution*, on a free and generous Plan," settling the dispute by "on the one side ascertaining and securing the liberties of the colonists, and on the other giving full weight and force to the supreme authority of the nation over all its dominions."[20]

In the fall of 1774, Galloway attempted to persuade the First Continental Congress to accept just such a constitutional arrangement. Although he failed to convince his fellow delegates that his scheme would adequately protect the colonists from further encroachment upon their rights, he did not then abandon the effort to work out a plan that would take the "genius, temper, and circumstances" of the American people into account and unite them with Britain "upon principles of English liberty." In all the proposals he offered over the next eight years, he insisted that the colonies had to be restored to their "antient and essential right of participating [in] the power of making the laws," for if they were not, then Parliament would be "as absolute and despotic over the Colonies, as any Monarch whatever who singly holds the legislative authority." Other loyalists who embarked upon the same venture of preparing reconciliation schemes exhibited an identical concern for American rights. John Randolph, the former attorney general of Virginia, asserted in 1780 that the Americans would be content only with "a Constitution, which will be satisfactory to them," and he defined this as one that granted to the colonies "the *sole* Power of Taxing themselves, & enacting such Laws, as they may think necessary for the ordering their internal Police." Similarly, Sir James Wright, the last royal governor of Georgia, declared in 1777 that "the only True Way to Conciliate and restore Harmony and affection again, and to Hold the Colonies to *Advantage*, will be by granting a Generous Plan or Constitution for America, and Settling the Mode of Taxation, on Some Clear Footing, so as not to admit of doubts or further disputes."[21]

The loyalists, then, did not oppose change within the empire; rather, they actively sought an alteration in the longstanding administrative and legislative practices of Great Britain. They, like their more radical compatriots, found fault with the way the empire was being run in the late 1760's and early 1770's, and they tried to find a means of correcting the flaws they perceived. They differed from their fellow Americans in the means of redress they preferred, but they were operating within the same whiggish framework and upon many of the same assumptions. This fact may be further demonstrated by taking a more detailed look at the exchanges between loyalists and revolutionaries printed in colonial pamphlets and newspapers during the crucial years 1774, 1775, and 1776.

2

Initially, the dispute took the form of a debate between orthodox Whigs and persons attempting to reinterpret traditional whiggish notions of government and politics. Throughout most of the decade following 1765, radical Americans devoted themselves to trying to find a formula for limiting the authority of Parliament over the colonies. As Bernard Bailyn has observed, the Americans' "central intellectual problem" was how to cope with the axiomatic 18th-century assumption that in every government there had to be one locus of supreme sovereign power, and that in the British Constitution that sovereignty rested with Parliament.[22] This assumption was the backbone of orthodox Whig thinking, and the radical colonists had to wrestle with it at every turn because of their desire to circumscribe parliamentary authority.

The loyalists, by contrast, had no such dilemma. They were arguing from a position of strength, for they could and did use the accepted principles of Whig thought to respond to claims that Parliament's power over the colonies could be restricted.

As Van Schaack correctly noted in 1776, once it was admitted that Americans and Britons were subjects of the same empire, Locke's "reasonings . . . will be found rather to militate against our claims; for he holds the necessity of a *supreme power,* and the necessary existence of *one legislature only* in every society, in the strongest terms." And the loyalists were certainly emphatic Lockeans on this point. "There is no position more firmly established, in the conduct of mankind, than that there must be in every State a supreme legislative authority, universal in its extent, over every member," wrote Galloway in 1775. He was echoed by such other authors as Seabury, Chandler, and George Chalmers, a Scottish lawyer who had emigrated to Maryland in the 1760's.[23]

The very idea that sovereignty could be divided or limited was an "absurdity"; indeed, it represented the fallacy the loyalists called *"imperium in imperio,"* or a government within a government. A political system "thus constituted," asserted Leonard, "would contain the seeds of dissolution in its first principles, and must soon destroy itself." Accordingly Leonard and the other loyalists early reached the conclusion that "there is no possible medium between absolute independence, and subjection to the authority of parliament."[24] It is exceedingly ironic but, on the other hand, perfectly understandable that many of the loyalists came to this realization months before some of their more radical countrymen did.

Both of the ways in which the radicals tried to restrict the authority of Parliament seemed equally ridiculous to loyalist writers. The older of the two was the notion that Parliament could legislate for, but not tax, the colonies, or that a line could be drawn between Parliament's internal and external regulating powers over America. This idea had first been tentatively advanced in 1765 and then carried to its height in John Dickinson's *Letters From a Pennsylvania Farmer* in 1767–68. By 1774, it had largely run its course, and so the loyalists dispatched it quickly.[25] Of more recent vintage, and therefore deserving more extensive treatment, was the radicals' claim that Americans were subject to the king but not to the Houses of Lords and Commons, which they had come to view as nothing more than a domestic British legislature. Leonard charged that such contentions demonstrated either "profound ignorance or hypocritical cunning." Since the king, Lords, and Commons constituted "but one supreme politic head" of the state, Galloway asserted, to say that one could "submit to the power of a *part*, and not to the *whole*, is too great an absurdity for men of sense to adopt."[26]

There was still another article of the radicals' creed that the loyalists found practically incomprehensible from the standpoint of traditional Whig thinking. This was the revolutionaries' strict application of the concept of consent. As Seabury put it, no one would deny that Englishmen were bound only by laws "to which the representatives of the nation have given their consent," but it was incorrect to interpret this as meaning that an Englishman was required to obey only those laws "to which *he* hath consented in person, or by *his* representative." Chandler emphasized that the maxim in question applied to "the nation *collectively*," and Peter Oliver pointed out that a man whose position was in the minority, or who did not vote, or whose chosen representative was not elected, was not in fact consenting to governmental measures. How then, he asked, could the requirement for consent be fulfilled?[27]

When the debate entered the phase in which independence and revolution were specifically at issue, persons on opposite sides of the dispute continued to frame their arguments in whiggish language. Contentions were made and answered on the basis of the same premises, and the participants used identical categories in their newspaper and pamphlet exchanges. One group of writers argued that the categories were applicable to the Americans' circumstances; the other group simply denied that fact. The colonists, it seems to me, were disagreeing over the relevancy of a set of ideas, rather than over the validity of those ideas.

As Pauline Maier has noted in her recent book, *From Resistance to Revolution*, the Americans and their intellectual forebears stressed restraint as well as resistance in their writings on the nature of revolution. They emphasized the right of the people to revolt against an unjust ruler, but at the same time they laid down regulations to guide that revolt. The most important of these rules were: first, that revolution could not be lightly undertaken, for the people's grievances had to be sufficient to justify such a drastic step. Second, that revolution was a last resort, to be used only when all other measures had failed. And third, that the people in question had to have good reason to believe that they would gain more than they would lose by a revolution.[28] Both loyalists and rebels subscribed to the belief that these conditions would have to be fulfilled before a legitimate revolution could occur. As a result, what they argued about in 1774–75 was whether the necessary circumstances for a revolution currently existed in the American colonies. Professors Maier and Bailyn have dealt in depth with the process through which many Americans came to the conclusion that a revolt was justifiable; my concern, therefore, is solely with the loyalists' opposite conclusion.

The loyalists directed a two-pronged attack at the notion that the Americans' grievances were sufficient to justify a revolution. Some writers argued than an "unhappy combination of untoward circumstances" had led Americans "to credit the most improbable stories, of designs, to deprive them of their rights and liberties." In fact, they contended, "nothing has been executed, or even attempted, by the mother country, . . . but what has been established by the repeated precedents of more than a century past." Certain actions of Parliament and the ministry had just been misinterpreted as being "unconstitutional" and unprecedented."[29] The loyalists did not deny that the British government had made mistakes in its dealings with the colonies, but, they observed, even the best of governments was liable to err on occasion. Because there was a "publick Confidence due from us to our Legislators . . . all just Allowances ought to be given to them, untill we can convince them, by Reason, of what is right." If they could not be persuaded of the truth, then they could be removed, but that was no reason for destroying the entire governmental structure, for the Americans, "like Samson, must be buried in its Ruins."[30]

The second line of argument was quite different. Relying on the experience of the years since 1765, some of the loyalists maintained that, since Parliament had previously proved receptive to American complaints about the Stamp Act and the Townshend duties, "what reason is there to suppose that government will not listen to us and to its own interest in this as well as in former instances?" They contended that the repeal of unwelcome laws in the past indicated that Britain was "ever attentive to the *real grievances* of her colonies" and that "a proper representation" of the colonial position would bring about a reversal of any policies thought to be "oppressive" and "generally disgustful to America."[31] Therefore, inquired Daniel Leonard, "are we to take up arms and make war against our parent, lest that parent, contrary to the experience of a century and a half, contrary to her own genius, inclination, affection and interest, should treat us or our posterity as bastards and not as sons, and instead of protecting should *enslave* us?"[32]

Even supposing that the Americans' grievances constituted adequate grounds for revolt, the loyalists stressed that violent steps could not be taken "till all legal and moderate ones have failed." Only after "mild and safe" tactics had been found to be "ineffectual" could actual resistance be justified.[33] And, they continued, the colonies had not yet reached that point. In fact, two viable alternatives to revolution had not so far been exhausted. The first was simply to have "recourse to our legal representatives," to depend upon the assemblies, "the proper guardians of our rights and liberties," rather than looking to the extralegal congresses and committees for a resolution of the current problems. If the assemblies unanimously petitioned Parliament on the subject of American grievances, Boucher declared, "it is hardly within the reach of supposition that all due attention will not be paid to their united remonstrances."[34]

Another difficulty with the colonists' previous efforts to win redress of their grievances was the tone of their petitions. Leonard charged in March 1775 that the recent American addresses to the authorities in Britain were "at once an insult to his majesty, and a libel on his government." Far from being "decent remonstrances," they were "insidious attempts to wrest from the crown, or the supreme legislature, their inherent, unalienable prerogatives or rights."[35] It was therefore understandable that the ministry had paid the colonists' pleas little heed, and the remedy was plain: change the contents of the petitions. Then and only then could the Americans expect to be heard sympathetically. What was needed, said Chandler, was "a formal allowance of the rightful supremacy in general, of *Great Britain*, over the American Colonies" coupled with "a respectful remonstrance on the subject of taxation" *and* "an assurance of our willingness to contribute, in some equitable proportion, towards defraying the public expences." If this were done, Seabury predicted, it would be highly likely that Britain would make "some concessions for peace-sake."[36]

Even if this argument could be disposed of, there remained still another line of defense against the cries for revolution, and that, in the loyalists' eyes, was perhaps the most potent of all. This was the assessment of the possible consequences of violent resistance to Great Britain. The loyalists first stressed the many benefits the colonies gained from their ties to the mother country: they had, after all, prospered and flourished under her protection and would undoubtedly continue to do so in the future if nothing disturbed the mutually advantageous relationship. By contrast, if the colonies rebelled, whether they were successful or unsuccessful, the revolt would "necessarily terminate in ruin and destruction." This was because civil war was a "two-edged" sword, "one of the severest scourges of Heaven," bringing devastation wherever it went.[37]

Indeed, declared the loyalists, it mattered not if the Americans won or lost the war, for they would be the losers in either case. Most likely, of course, they would be defeated, because war was an "intricate science," learned only from the sort of "long experience" that the colonists so obviously lacked. The future the loyalists foresaw was terrible: "our Cities destroyed our fields uncultivated our Plains strewed with death and Ruin." And all for what? "Why to be enslaved at last," to become "a conquered people, subject to such laws as the conquerors shall think proper to impose," with "all our rights and privileges forfeited."[38] In other words, failure, the probable result of a revolution, would put the Americans in a far less desirable state than they currently enjoyed.

And the colonists could not possibly gain even if they won their independence. If "by any miraculous event" they should achieve their "mad design," they would soon become "a prey to a foreign power," most likely one controlled by "the slavery and superstition of Rome." As a result they would lose not only their civil freedom but their religious liberty as well. Moreover, without the guiding hand of Britain, "we should soon see province waging war against province," even man against man. "Destruction and carnage would dessolate the land," Seabury predicted, and Leonard suggested that "some aspiring genius" would then take advantage of the "enfeebled, bleeding, and distracted state of the colonies" to "subjugate the whole to the yoke of despotism." No wonder that Charles Inglis wrote of independence: "I stand aghast at the prospect—my blood runs chill when I think of the calamities, the complicated evils that must ensue."[39]

The loyalists' message was unmistakable: the Americans' grievances were inadequate to justify such a violent act as rebellion; the colonists had not yet explored all avenues short of revolt; and, in any case, they could not benefit from seeking independence, whether they won or lost. Like the good Whigs they were, the loyalists had examined the proper whiggish conditions for revolution and pronounced them wanting in America. And some of them made this chain of reasoning quite explicit.

For example, when William Smith was called before the New York Council of Safety in 1777 and asked whether he considered himself to be a subject of his state government, he replied that he still regarded himself as "a Member of the old or British Government" because he "never thought the Seperation justifiable." Why? He believed that "Resistance to Governmt. could never be innocent unless there was great Oppression & Revolution [was] practicable and the Remedy sure." There had to be a "Moral Certainty" that the "Evils" of revolution would be less than the evils that had caused the revolt. And this he denied. It seemed to him that "a Seperation from Great Britain could not be contended for with Safety to the Rights Liberties and Privileges of this Country," and consequently he felt compelled to oppose independence.[40]

Likewise, Peter Van Schaack carefully studied the problem in whiggish terms before reaching a decision on his allegiance. "That legitimate governments should be supported, and that tyranny may be opposed, are principles equally incontestable," Van Schaack declared, "but what in fact is the one or the other, is left to the private judgement of every individual." In Van Schaack's considered opinion, the parliamentary acts "complained of" by his compatriots did not "manifest a system of slavery," but rather could be "imputed to human frailty, and the difficulty of the subject." Some were solidly based on precedent, others had "sprung out of particular occasions" and appeared to be "unconnected with each other." Although some of the laws were unwise, they had probably been passed "without a preconcerted plan of enslaving us." Accordingly, he concluded in pure Lockean fashion, "I cannot therefore think the government *dissolved*; and as long as the society lasts, the power that every individual gave the society when he entered into it, can never revert to the individuals again, but will always remain in the community."[41]

By late 1774, the traditionally minded loyalists were finding their opponents' ideas so strange that they began casting about for a possible explanation for the absurdities of their fellow countrymen's position. Oliver and Seabury eventually hit upon an answer that seemed plausible to them. The Members of the First Continental Congress, declared Oliver, had "sacrificed their Understandings, in Order to make themselves of Consequence in a Republick." Seabury asserted that the division drawn between the king and Parliament was a "distinction made by the American Republicans to serve their own rebellious purposes." Furthermore, he contended, the radicals' interpretation of the requirement for consent was "republican in its very nature, and tends to the utter subversion of the English monarchy."[42] At long last the crux of the difficulty had been exposed. The radicals were not Whigs at all, the loyalists charged: they were republicans. The Continental Congress, said Seabury, was the beginning of "a grand American Republic." Moreover, the loyalists recognized with the advantages of hindsight that the Americans' plans for a republic had been "long projected." In March 1775, for example, a Boston Anglican cleric wrote knowingly to his superior that "the general disposition of these New Eng. Colonys is now & ever has been republican."[43]

Looking back, the loyalists could now perceive that "some of the first settlers in America" had held "hereditary wrong principles." Galloway commented that the "two great objects" of the Pilgrims' migration to America had been "an independent church, and a republican society." Under no restraint from England, they had been able to institute both, and their lead had been followed by the later colonizers of Massachusetts Bay. The republicanism of New England had then spread throughout the American continent, as emigrants from that crowded region settled elsewhere and took their principles with them.[44] The pattern, or so the loyalists thought, was undeniable.

Now that the true nature of the dispute had been revealed, the loyalists knew how to deal with it. The contest was one between whiggery and republicanism, and so they marshaled the usual Whig arguments to use against the ancient republican heresy. "Liberty cannot exist for any time, where the supreme power of a state is not divided," wrote Charles Inglis confidently. "The Government of a great Nation must provide as well for checking the Wantoness of the Populace as for restraining the Pride of the Magistracy," agreed William Smith, and the only way to accomplish this was "by classing the Rich and giving them Powers of Defence—a Legislature of Beggars will be Thieves." It was dangerous, Smith warned, "to admit Persons with very small Property to participate in your Councils." Since the poor constituted the vast majority of the population, they "ought not to refuse a Security to others against the Spoil of their Property—They lose Nothing by being obliged to elect Men of Substance attached to the Territory."[45]

In addition to the problem posed by the lack of a properly balanced government, the loyalists foresaw difficulties stemming from the size of the proposed American republic. For centuries political theorists had postulated that republics could survive only if they were small. To Inglis, it was obvious that America was "too unwieldy for the feeble, dilatory ad-

ministration of democracy." Again Smith agreed; he thought even the
state of Pennsylvania too large to exist as an "unmixed Republic," and he
expressed his firm conviction that it was "excessively absurd for large
Countries to set out with that Form of Governmt."[46]

When the loyalists looked around themselves in late 1774 and early 1775,
they found abundant evidence that their fears of the dangers of republican
government were well founded. The Continental Congress and its allied
committees had established a "system of lawless tyranny," a "despotism
cruelly carried into execution by mobs and riots." Americans were being
reduced to a state of "abject slavery," they told their fellow countrymen;
the colonists were being forced to surrender their "liberty and property to
an illegal, tyrannical Congress" and to submit to "a body of men unchecked, uncontrouled by the civil power." The worst of the loyalists' whiggish predictions were beginning to come true.[47]

3

It might well be asked at this point what the significance is of this extended exercise in the analysis of political terminology. Does it matter
whether the loyalists are called Whigs or Tories? Are they not still the
same people, expressing the same sentiments? The answer to this last question is, of course, yes, but there is much to be gained from putting the
loyalists into a Whig perspective, where they rightfully belong. For one
thing, it means that they can be interpreted as participants in the regular
course of American development in the 18th century rather than as inex-
plicable anomalies. For another, it means that there will be less chance of
the loyalists being seen as monolithically conservative "Tories," as unthinking supporters of monarchical prerogatives, and as villains who willfully
betrayed the best interests of their country. More importantly still, however,
it means that historical questions that have been shaped by the traditional
Tory-Whig dichotomy can be reshaped and asked in different and more
useful ways.

To cite just one example: for years historians have been asking, "What
would lead a man to become a loyalist?" From the very outset that question is biased, because the implicit assumption is that being a revolutionary
was the "normal" thing and that being a loyalist was the aberration. No
matter; the question was asked and answered most successfully by William

Nelson, in his 1961 book *The American Tory*. Nelson suggests a number of reasons for loyalism, among them governmental connections by appointment or kinship, residence in the back country (with a concomitant distrust of the intentions of the inhabitants of the seaboard), and membership in a religious or cultural minority group that felt threatened by a ruling majority.[48]

There is nothing in Nelson's schema to tie any of these factors together, and yet when they are seen in the light of the loyalists' whiggery, a link among them immediately appears.

For if, as I have argued, both loyalists and revolutionaries were Whigs, what then was the significant ideological difference between the two groups? It seems to be the fact that the loyalists adhered to orthodox Whig thought and the revolutionaries chose rather to modify that thought in ways that then led them into republicanism. The loyalists usually envisioned republicanism as a disease or poison that had managed to infect the body politic,[49] and their metaphor is useful in explaining my point. If we conceive the problem in approximately the same manner, that is, seeing the loyalists as for some reason *immune* to the republican poison, resistant to the diseased strain of whiggery, the connection between Nelson's categories quickly emerges. The question needs only to be phrased in this manner: what was it that prevented certain men from being carried away by the radical rhetoric that charged the British ministry, Parliament, and the king with connivance at a plan to enslave the colonies?

Upon examination, each of the groups identified by Nelson has a particular characteristic that at least tended to supply immunity to radical ideas. Men who held royal office, who participated in the governing process, who were often in relatively close contact with superiors in England, had good reason to be skeptical of claims that there was a deliberate conspiracy afoot to destroy American rights. For example, Thomas Hutchinson, who was accused of taking part in the plot himself, was genuinely dumbfounded and bewildered by the charges thrown at him. He knew he was not part of a conspiracy against the colonies; no wonder, then, that he categorically rejected the whole notion. Or, to take another of Nelson's categories: men who had been long-time opponents of American radicals for other reasons, whether those reasons were religious or cultural persecution, political rivalries, or economic competition, already distrusted the radicals. Why should such men believe the extravagant statements about a ministerial plot? Further, the main vehicles for the transmittal of the revolutionaries' ideas were the newspapers of the port cities. Is it not logical to suppose that persons in the back country of the Carolinas or Virginia only rarely saw such publications? Not having been exposed to the "disease," how could they catch it?[50]

There is, moreover, another insight that can be gained from handling the inquiry into the loyalists' motivations in this manner. It has been argued throughout this paper that most loyalists can be characterized both as Whigs and as persons generally sympathetic to American protests against certain British policies. What of the exceptions? I would suggest that men who were not both Whigs and American sympathizers were probably most resistant of all to the radicals' notions. Either, like Jonathan Boucher, they repudiated Whig ideas, or, like many recent immigrants, they had not yet developed a sufficient attachment to the colonies to feel a unity with other Americans. In either case it is entirely logical and understandable that the persons in question remained loyal to the crown.

In light of the argument I have advanced, there seems to be no better way to conclude this paper than with a quotation from William Smith. When in 1777 Smith was chided by his friend James Duane for his failure to embrace republicanism, he replied, "If you wanted a New Governmt. it should have been on the British Model. I am a Whigg of the old Stamp. No Roundhead—one of King Wm's Whiggs, for Liberty & the Constitution."[51] That statement, I would contend, could just as accurately have been made by almost every other loyalist.

Notes

¹ See Wallace Brown, *The King's Friends* (Providence, Brown University Press, 1965). For an earlier view, cf. Moses Coit Tyler, "The Party of the Loyalists in the American Revolution," *American Historical Review*, 1(1895):24–45.

² On Toryism in England: J. H. Plumb, *The Origins of Political Stability in England, 1675–1725* (Boston, Houghton Mifflin, 1967), esp. p. 151; Jeffrey Hart, *Viscount Bolingbroke, Tory Humanist* (London, Routledge & K. Paul, 1965), esp. p. 29–30; Keith Grahame Feiling, *The Second Tory Party 1714–1832* (London, Macmillan and Co., Ltd., 1938), esp. p. 1–12.

³ Jonathan Boucher, *A View of the Causes and Consequences of the American Revolution* ... (London, Printed for G. G. & J. Robinson, 1797), p. xxii; John Adams and Jonathan Sewall (i.e., Daniel Leonard), *Novanglus and Massachusettensis* ... (reprint, New York, Russell & Russell, 1968), p. 149, 225–226. For an observation similar to Leonard's, see George Chalmers, *Political Annals of the Present United Colonies* ... (reprint, New York, Burt Franklin, 1968), vol. 1, p. 674.

⁴ See Plumb, *Origins of Political Stability*, p. 134–135, on the constitutional principles of English Whigs.

⁵ On the development of American revolutionary ideology: Bernard Bailyn, *The Ideological Origins of the American Revolution* (Cambridge, Harvard University Press, 1967); Gordon S. Wood, *The Creation of the American Republic, 1776–1787* (Chapel Hill, University of North Carolina Press, 1969); and Pauline Maier, *From Resistance to Revolution* (New York, Alfred A. Knopf, 1972).

⁶ William A. Benton argues this point in his *Whig-Loyalism* (Rutherford, N.J., Fairleigh-Dickinson University Press, 1969).

⁷ See, e.g., Bailyn, *Ideological Origins*, p. 28–29.

⁸ [Joseph Galloway], *Political Reflections on the late Colonial Governments* . . . (London, Printed for G. Wilkie, 1783), p. 2; Jacob Duché, *The Duty of Standing Fast in Our Spiritual and Temporal Liberties*. . . (Philadelphia, Printed & sold by J. Humphreys, Junior, 1775), p. 12; [Isaac Hunt], *The Political Family*. . . (Philadelphia, Printed by James Humphreys, Junior, 1775), p. 7–8; Daniel Batwell, *A Sermon, preached at Yorktown*. . . *on Thursday, July 20, 1775*. . . (Philadelphia, Printed by John Dunlap, 1775), p. 14. It should be noted, though, that in *A Candid Examination of the Mutual Claims of Great Britain, and the Colonies*. . . (London, Republished by G. Wilkie and R. Faulder, 1780) [originally published in New York by James Rivington, 1775], p. 87–90, Galloway specifically denied the proposition that Locke's theory of the social compact applied to the settlement of the colonies.

⁹ Samuel Seabury, *Letters of a Westchester Farmer*. . ., ed. Clarence H. Vance (White Plains, N.Y., Published for Westchester County by the Westchester County Historical Society, 1930), p. 109; Charles Inglis, claims memorial, Feb. 10, 1784, Audit Office 12, vol. 20, f 370, Public Record Office, London (hereafter cited as AO and PRO). For the revolutionaries' definition of civil liberty: Bailyn, *Ideological Origins*, p. 77; Maier, *From Resistance to Revolution*, p. 29–30. Other examples of similar definitions in loyalist writings may be found in [Thomas Bradbury Chandler], *What Think Ye of the Congress Now?*. . . (New York, Printed by James Rivington, 1775), p. 7; Peter Oliver, *Origin & Progress of the American Rebellion*. . ., ed. Douglass Adair and John A. Schutz (San Marino, Calif., Huntington Library, 1961), p. 4–6; and William H. W. Sabine, ed., *Historical Memoirs from 12 July 1776 to 25 July 1778 of William Smith*. . . (New York, 1958), p. 18 (hereafter cited as Sabine, ed., *Smith Diary*, vol. 2).

¹⁰ [Thomas Bradbury Chandler], *A Friendly Address to All Reasonable Americans*. . . (New York, Printed by J. Rivington, 1774), p. 9–10. Cf. John Locke, *Two Treatises of Government*, ed. Peter Laslett (New York and Toronto, 1965), p. 402–404 (hereafter cited as Laslett, ed., *Locke Treatises*). Interestingly enough, Chandler thought he was taking issue with Locke. And see Adams and Leonard, *Novanglus and Massachusettensis*, p. 202.

¹¹ Henry C. Van Schaack, *The Life of Peter Van Schaack* . . . (New York, D. Appleton & Co., 1842), p. 54; Thomas Hutchinson to —, Feb. 1775, Egerton Manuscripts 2661, f. 118, British Museum, London. Also, "Phileirene," *Boston News-Letter*, Jan. 12, 1775; Duché, *Duty*, p. 13. Alexander Hewatt, the loyalist author of *An Historical Account of the Rise and Progress of the Colonies of South Carolina and Georgia*, 2 vols. (Spartanburg, S.C., Reprint Co., 1962) used this sort of reasoning to justify the revolt of the Carolinians against the proprietors of their colony in the early 18th century (*Historical Account*, vol. 1, p. 291–295).

[12] Galloway, *Candid Examination*, p. 21. Cf. *ibid.*, p. 33.

[13] Boucher, *View*, p. 519–520, 525, 545, 498.

[14] *Ibid.*, p. lxvi, 593, 546. Also, 209.

[15] *Ibid.*, p. 422–423, 363. Also, 482, 509, 552. Other loyalists who wrote tirades against rebellion also qualified their statements by the use of the term "lawful" or "rightful" government; see Oliver, *Origin & Progress*, p. 161; and Myles Cooper, *National Humilation and Repentance Recommended* . . . (Oxford, Clarendon Press, 1777), p. 12.

[16] Chandler, *Congress*, p. 7; Anne Y. Zimmer and Alfred H. Kelly, "Jonathan Boucher: Constitutional Conservative," *Journal of American History*, 58(Mar. 1972): 897–910.

[17] William H. W. Sabine, ed., *Historical Memoirs from 16 March 1763 to 9 July 1776 of William Smith...* (New York, 1956), p. 272–274, 276 (hereafter cited as Sabine, ed., *Smith Diary*, vol. 1). Also, on the Stamp Act: Thomas Hutchinson, "Defence of his Conduct 1764–1774," Thomas Hutchinson Papers, Massachusetts Historical Society, Boston; Chandler, *Friendly Address*, p. 45; Adams and Leonard, *Novanglus and Massachusettensis*, p. 147.

[18] Van Schaack, *Life*, p. 28, 23–24. And, Jacob Duché, *The American Vine,...* (Philadelphia, Printed by James Humphreys, Junior, 1775), p. 21; Duché, *Duty*, p. 15.

[19] Galloway, *Candid Examination*, p. 60; "Letters of Rev. Jonathan Boucher 1759–1777," *Maryland Historical Magazine*, 8(1913):338–339.

[20] Chandler, *Friendly Address*, p. 47; Seabury, *Letters*, p. 73. For similar formulations: "New York Freeholder," *Boston News-Letter*, Nov. 10, 1774 (supplement); Adams and Leonard, *Novanglus and Massachusettensis*, p. 202; Sabine, ed., *Smith Diary*, vol. 2, p. 7.

[21] Galloway, *Candid Examination*, p. 53–54, 86; Mary Beth Norton, ed., "John Randolph's 'Plan of Accommodations,'" *William and Mary Quarterly*, 3d ser., 28(Jan. 1971):107, 112; Sir James Wright, "Notes on Considering the State of Affairs in America," Feb. 12, 1777, Germain Papers, William L. Clements Library, Ann Arbor.

[22] Bailyn, *Ideological Origins*, p. 198–202.

[23] Van Schaack, *Life*, p. 55; Galloway, *Candid Examination*, p. 10; Seabury, *Letters*, p. 110–111; Chandler, *Friendly Address*, p. 8; Chalmers, *Political Annals*, vol. 1, p. 672. Cf. Laslett, ed., *Locke Treatises*, p. 401, 413–414.

[24] Adams and Leonard, *Novanglus and Massachusettensis*, p. 198, 174. Also, [Thomas B. Chandler], *The American Querist...* (New York, Printed by James Rivington, 1774), p. 5–7; Anthony Stokes, *A View of the Constitution of the British Colonies...* (London, Printed for the author and sold by B. White, 1783), p. 146.

[25] See, e.g., Seabury, *Letters*, p. 117. But William Smith did think the distinction useful (Sabine, ed., *Smith Diary*, vol. 1, p. 228–228a).

[26] Adams and Leonard, *Novanglus and Massachusettensis*, p. 181; Galloway, *Candid Examination*, p. 14. And, Seabury, *Letters*, p. 112; "Plainheart," *Boston News-Letter*, Feb. 16, 1775.

27 Seabury, *Letters*, p. 111; Chandler, *Querist*, p. 22; Oliver, *Origin & Progress*, p. 7–8. Intriguingly, Chandler in *What Think Ye of the Congress Now* used the revolutionaries' concept of consent to attack the legitimacy of the First Continental Congress (see esp. p. 6, 17–18).

28 Maier, *From Resistance to Revolution*, p. 28–42.

29 "Plainheart," *Boston News-Letter*, Feb. 16, 1775; "Phileirene," *ibid.*, Jan. 12, 1775. Also, "Phileirene's" essays in *ibid.*, March 2, 9, 30, 1775; Adams and Leonard, *Novanglus and Massachusettensis*, p. 192–195; Chandler, *Friendly Address*, p. 19–21.

30 Oliver, *Origin & Progress*, p. 9. Also, Boucher, *View*, p. 417; "C," *Boston News-Letter*, Feb. 16, 1775.

31 "New York Freeholder," *Boston News-Letter*, Nov. 10, 1774 (supplement); Adams and Leonard, *Novanglus and Massachusettensis*, p. 212, 147, 218.

32 Adams and Leonard, *Novanglus and Massachusettensis*, p. 217. On lessons to be learned from the Stamp Act repeal: Boucher, *View*, p. 417–418; Hunt, *Political Family*, p. 12; Seabury, *Letters*, p. 128–129; Chandler, *Querist*, p. 17–19.

33 Seabury, *Letters*, p. 96; Chandler, *Congress*, p. 42. Also, "New York Freeholder," *Boston News-Letter*, Nov. 10, 1774 (supplement).

34 Chandler, *Congress*, p. 42; [Isaac Wilkins], *Short Advice to the Counties of New-York* . . . (New York, Printed by James Rivington, 1774), p. 7; Boucher, *View*, p. 558. And, Seabury, *Letters*, p. 66, 120.

35 Adams and Leonard, *Novanglus and Massachusettensis*, p. 218. Also, Galloway, *Candid Examination*, p. 61–62; Seabury, *Letters*, p. 73.

36 Chandler, *Friendly Address*, p. 46; Seabury, *Letters*, p. 138. See Chandler, *Congress*, p. 15–16, for a more detailed statement of Chandler's position.

37 Chandler, *Friendly Address*, p. 47–48; Cooper, *National Humiliation*, p. 10. On American prosperity: Adams and Leonard, *Novanglus and Massachusettensis*, p. 210–217.

38 Adams and Leonard, *Novanglus and Massachusettensis*, p. 226; Henry H. Ferguson to Benjamin Rush, June 8, 1775, AO 13, vol. 102, pt. 2, f 750, PRO; Galloway, *Candid Examination*, p. 59. Also, [James Chalmers], *Plain Truth* . . . (London, 1776), passim; "Phileirene," *Boston News-Letter*, Jan. 26, 1775.

39 Galloway, *Candid Examination*, p. 59–60; Seabury, *Letters*, p. 99; Adams and Leonard, *Novanglus and Massachusettensis*, p. 185; [Charles Inglis], *The True Interest of America* . . . (Philadelphia, Printed and sold by James Humphreys, 1776), p. 49. Also, Chandler, *Friendly Address*, p. 26; *Letters and Papers of John Singleton Copley and Henry Pelham 1739–1776; Collections of the Massachusetts Historical Society*, vol. 71 (Boston, 1914), p. 351.

40 Sabine, ed., *Smith Diary*, vol. 2, p. 154, 156.

41 Van Schaack, *Life*, p. 86, 56–57.

42 Oliver, *Origin & Progress*, p. 135; Seabury, *Letters*, p. 98, 111.

43 Seabury, *Letters*, p. 96; Chandler, *Friendly Address*, p. 29; Henry Caner to the Archbishop of London, Mar. 27, 1775, Caner Letterbook, University of Bristol Library,

Bristol, England. For more information on this use of republicanism, see W. Paul Adams, "Republicanism in Political Rhetoric before 1776," *Political Science Quarterly*, 85(1970):397–421.

[44] Boucher, *View*, p. 472; [Joseph Galloway], *Historical and Political Reflections on the Rise and Progress of the American Rebellion...* (London, Printed for G. Wilkie, 1780), p. 27–30; Hewatt, *Historical Account*, vol. 2, p. 308–309; Sabine, ed., *Smith Diary*, vol. 2, p. 8. Cf. Michael Kammen, "The Meaning of Colonization in American Revolutionary Thought," *Journal of the History of Ideas*, 31(1970):337–358.

[45] [Charles Inglis], *The Letters of Papinian:...* (New York, Printed by H. Gaine, 1779), p. 120; Sabine, ed., *Smith Diary*, vol. 2, p. 23–24, 18.

[46] Inglis, *True Interest*, p. 53; Sabine, ed., *Smith Diary*, vol. 2, p. 23; Leslie Francis Stokes Upton, ed., *The Diary and Selected Papers of Chief Justice William Smith 1784–1793* (Toronto, Champlain Society, 1963), vol. 1, p. 153. See W. Paul Adams, "Republicanism in Political Rhetoric before 1776," *Political Science Quarterly*, 85(1970): 412–418, for further loyalist arguments against republicanism.

[47] *Pills for the Delegates* (New York, James Rivington, 1775), p. 31; Adams and Leonard, *Novanglus and Massachusettensis*, p. 158; Seabury, *Letters*, p. 61, 87, 86.

[48] William H. Nelson, *The American Tory* (New York, Oxford University Press, 1961), passim. esp. p. 85–92.

[49] See, e.g., Hewatt, *Historical Account*, vol. 2, p. 329; Adams and Leonard, *Novanglus and Massachusettensis*, p. 156; Galloway, *Historical and Political Reflections*, p. 115.

[50] The idea of distance as a factor was suggested by Prof. Pauline Maier.

[51] Sabine, ed., *Smith Diary*, vol. 2, p. 278.

Esmond Wright is director of the Institute of United States Studies and professor of American history at the University of London. He holds degrees from the University of Virginia as well as from King's College, Newcastle, and has taught at Glasgow University and Strathclyde University. During World War II, he served in the Middle East, attaining the rank of lieutenant-colonel.

In 1967 Professor Wright was elected to Parliament as a Conservative Party Member from Glasgow, Pollok. During his three years in Parliament he served on the House of Commons Select Committee on Scottish Affairs and the Select Committee on Education and Science and was chairman of the Scottish Sub-committee.

Professor Wright's publications include A Short History of Our Own Times, 1919–1950 *(1951),* Washington and the American Revolution *(1957),* Fabric of Freedom, 1763–1800 *(1961),* Benjamin Franklin and American Independence *(1966),* American Profiles *(1967), and* A Time for Courage *(1971). He has also served as editor of various historical volumes and has contributed numerous articles on the Revolutionary War period.*

AFTER HEARING Professor Norton's paper I think perhaps we should consider a new name for the Tories. Why not call them the "Conscience Whigs"?

It is indeed appropriate that a British scholar should act as commentator of Miss Norton's paper, for one of the extraordinary aspects of the scholarship of American history in the last few decades has been the fact that it has now come into its own abroad—both on the European continent and in England, which has given us a veritable galaxy of distinguished Americanists. One of them, Esmond Wright, has very special qualifications, as evidenced by his splendid selection of essays on *The Causes and Consequences of the American Revolution*, his *Fabric of Freedom,* and his insightful studies of Franklin and Washington. But to add to his special qualifications as a commentator, until recently he was a Conservative Member of Parliament. Just think if we could have had a Tory Member of Parliament debate the issues at the First Continental Congress! What a wonderful confrontation we would have had.

Men With Two Countries

ESMOND WRIGHT

PROF. MARY BETH NORTON is to be congratulated on her paper, which is both well informed and well researched, as one would expect of a student of Bernard Bailyn now teaching at the late Clinton Rossiter's university, and who has steeped herself in Thomas Hutchinson's London and in his papers at the British Museum. Indeed the quality of her research is unobtrusive, since this is the second edition of her paper—she has been revising it very steadily over the last three weeks. The organizers of this conference are also to be congratulated, for they have well brought out the contrapuntal quality of the argument of the Revolution. For there was a genuine dialectic in 1776—there was a case for and a case against. This point is best made perhaps by quoting the opening words of a recent study, *The Politics of Revolution,* by Harvey Wheeler. He writes:

"It was the best of times. It was the worst of times." This opening theme of Dickens'

Tale of Two Cities might be taken as the theme of all revolutions, for all revolutions are tales of two cities, tales of societies that have divided in two. . . . Revolution is not a storming of the palace gates; it is not the Weathermen bombing a bank; it is the dialectic of two competing cultural sytems warring against each other in the same society.[1]

I endorse what Mary Beth Norton says, that in essence, "Tory" is not a word for scholars. Most Tories were "rather ordinary" people, "not very different from their revolutionary compatriots." The American Tory was a Whig par excellence, upholder of 1688. "It was the American revolutionaries who in the imperial world were the aberrations."

They were not Jacobites seeking to perpetuate the Stuart line—though for interest she might have pointed to the oddity that some ex-Jacobites did fight in North Carolina for George III, grandson of the Auld Enemy. And they were not Tories, she says, "in the traditional English sense of the term"—a somewhat ambiguous phrase, since the word Tory is Irish (the word Whig is Scottish, referring to the Covenanters of 1648), not English, and connotes "outlaws or armed Irish Papists."

But the intellectual conflict was, she says, between Whig and Whig, the old Whig and the new, to use Burke's language.

Professor Norton puts the point in another way in saying that Whigs and Tories alike were all Lockeans. Here she could have invoked earlier commentators; thus, Gentleman Johnny Burgoyne:

I am no stranger to the Doctrines of Mr. Locke and other of the best advocates for the rights of mankind, upon the compact always implied between the governing and the governed, and the right of resistance in the latter, when the compact shall be so violated as to leave no other means of redress. I look with reverence almost amounting to idolatry upon those immortal whigs who adopted and applied such doctrine during part of the reign of Charles I and in that of James II.

Or, with a novel twist, take the Hessian captain Johann Heinrichs writing in January 1778:

Call this war, dearest friend, by whatsoever name you may, only call it not an American Rebellion, it is nothing more or less than an Irish-Scotch Presbyterian Rebellion.

Indeed it is probable that *Cato's Letters* was far more important than Locke anyway. When Thomas Gordon and John Trenchard collaborated on *Cato's Letters* in the 1720's, they chose Cato because he had "contended for public liberty and freedom," and they commented on the meaninglessness of party labels and explained the obsession with power: "A Tory under oppression or out of place is a Whig; a Whig with power to oppress

is a Tory." There had been, they said, a time when the word "Tory" con-
noted an extreme royalist, but by the 18th century power and the pursuit
of it had obliterated principle: "No men upon earth have been more servile
crouching and abandoned creatures of power than the Whigs sometimes
have been."

And in England more important than Locke or Trenchard and Gordon
was Sir William Blackstone—his first volume of *Commentaries on the
Laws of England* was published in 1765:

> There is and must be in every state a supreme irresistible absolute and uncontrolled
> authority in which the *jura summa imperii* or rights of sovereignty reside, and this
> supreme power is by the constitution of Great Britain vested in the King Lords and
> Commons.

The Tories, in other words, cited Locke for one reason—to emphasize
the supremacy of the crown in Parliament and of Parliament against the
crown. The Whigs cited Locke for another, with their local colonial assemblies in mind, and it was for these that they demanded liberty. But this
was a distortion, because the authority Locke supported was that of the
British Parliament.

When the issue was squarely raised by the Whigs, the Tories stated flatly
their position—two independent legislatures cannot exist in the same state.
Or as Isaac Hunt put the proposition:

> Two distinct *independent powers* in *one civil state* are as inconsistent as *two hearts* in
> the same natural body. . . . A due subordination of the less parts to the greater is
> therefore necessary to the *existence* of BOTH.

The empire was thus viewed by the Tories as a single state, geograph-
ically but not politically divided, with its government established by the
Constitution of 1688; to deny the established authority of any part of that
government was to destroy the whole. Daniel Leonard clearly saw, as he
wrote in 1774, that to deny the authority of Parliament was to destroy the
framework of the Constitution and with it the "priceless claim" to all the
rights guaranteed by that Constitution. On the same reasoning, Samuel
Seabury labeled the Whig contention that the colonists owed allegiance not
to Parliament but to the king a self-contradictory heresy:

> It is a distinction made by the American republicans to serve their own rebellious pur-
> poses,—a gilding with which they have enclosed the pill of sedition. . . . The king of
> Great Britain was placed on the throne by virtue of an act of parliament. . . . And if
> we disclaim that authority of parliament which made him our king, we, in fact, reject
> him from being our king,—for we disclaim that authority by which he is king at all.

The year 1649 may be significant. To Great Britain, 1688 was even more so, when it was realized that it was not necessary to cut off a king's head to guarantee political liberty. To Tories, British government was that of *King-in-Parliament* and not that of monarchy alone.

But in seeing Tories as old Whigs, Mary Beth Norton is properly worried over Boucher, whom she sees correctly as an authoritarian and not a Whig at all. And she quotes him as saying: "All Government is in its nature absolute and irresistible."

But there were many others like him. Professor Norton, by concentrating on the intellectual arguments of the loyalists, minimizes the character and extent of the religious roots of Toryism. It was religious as well as political, and perhaps less sophisticated than she implies. Boucher himself paid tribute to the loyalist in his *View of the Causes and Consequences of the American Revolution* by adapting lines of *Paradise Lost:*

> Among the faithless faithful chiefly they—
> Among innumerable false unmov'd,
> Unshaken, unseduc'd, unterrified,
> Their *loyalty* they kept, their love, their zeal:
> Nor number, nor example, with them wrought,
> To swerve from truth, or change their constant mind.

The Anglican clergy were in a special position. They had a special connection with British authority; many of them were born in the British Isles; all of them had been ordained there; those who were missionaries of the Society for the Propagation of the Gospel received all or part of their incomes from England; and all of them, like the officials of government, were bound by special oaths of allegiance and obedience to their king. It is not to be wondered at that a large proportion of them remained either actively or passively loyal to the mother country in the struggle. To quote the Reverend Ebeneezer Diblee of Stamford, Conn. (October 28, 1765), they sought:

both in public and private, to inculcate the great duty of obedience and subjection to the government in being, and steadfast adherence to that well tempered frame of polity upon which this Protestant Church of ours is built, a constitution happily balanced between tyranny and anarchy.

Or the Reverend Dr. George Micklejohn of North Carolina, who in the Regulator troubles declared firmly that the powers that be are ordained of God and that "subjection to lawful authority is one plain and principal doctrine of Christianity." In other words, Boucher is not unique. The line might be between one form of Whiggism and another. It was also, and more sharply, between Anglican and Dissenter. The parallel is not only with 1688 and 1649, but with the Act of Supremacy of 1532, or with 1604 —"No Bishop, no King." Similar sentiments were voiced by Samuel Seabury of Westchester, by Myles Cooper and Charles Inglis of New York, and by Thomas Bradbury Chandler of Elizabethtown, N.J.

So much for what Professor Norton says.

Let me note what can only be called additions to her loyalist canon, footnotes to her discourse.

However "ordinary" loyalism's following, as a cause it was conservative, the creed of the friends of government. It was sectionalist—and hundreds signed loyalist petitions in the Regulator country of North Carolina. And it had a reverential and a Burkean note, as well as a Lockean, a note of secular as well as Anglican authoritarianism. Take Martin Howard, in his *Letter from a Gentleman at Halifax* (1766), and note the parallels with Burke:

> The goodly building of the British constitution will be best secured and perpetuated by adhering to its original principles. Parliaments are not of yesterday; they are as ancient as our Saxon ancestors. Why should the beauty and symmetry of this body be destroyed and its purity defiled by the unnatural mixture of representatives from every part of the British dominions? What a heterogeneous council would this form? What a monster in government would it be? In truth, my friend, the matter lies here: the freedom and happiness of every British subject depends not upon his share in elections but upon the sense and virtue of the British Parliament, and these depend reciprocally upon the sense and virtue of the whole nation. When virtue and honor are no more, the lovely frame of our constitution will be dissolved. Britain may one day be what Athens and Rome now are; but may Heaven long protract the hour!

There was a real fear of anarchy, of civil war and civil confusion and the "two-edged sword"; independence and slavery, some said, were synonymous terms. The recollections of the Levellers and 1649 did not bring pleasure to everyone. Some preferred the will of a remote British ministry to the will of a New York committee. This was, in contrast to enlightened Europe, a liberal empire: in 1760, of 31 subordinate governments in the British Empire, 21 had some form of representative institution. Pride as well as prejudice was part of loyalism.

And there is one striking omission from Professor Norton's paper, because of its absence from the Tory view. All other Tories in history have been profoundly historically minded and this has been part strength, part weakness. What is striking about the American Tories is that they do *not* invoke an American past, and for the Whigs—as Professor Commager reminded us—the past was prologue. In Europe—especially in France in 1789

—history, the past, was seen as the enemy, especially to Voltaire and Condorcet. History in America was, insofar as it mattered, on the side of the Whigs.

Or as Gordon Wood puts it: "The Americans were not an oppressed people; they had no crushing imperial shackles to throw off." So that, as he notes, Tories found the Revolution frankly incomprehensible. Never in history, said Daniel Leonard, had there been so much rebellion with so "little real cause"; or as Peter Oliver put it, it was "the most wanton and unnatural rebellion that ever existed."

I do not find many studies catching this flavor of the real incomprehensibility of the Revolution. It is not in my view explicable merely by tracing its intellectual roots, nor in isolation from the counterarguments of the loyalists.

I accept Professor Norton's thesis that the loyalists were Whigs rather than Tories. They were not just a landed class but a wide cross section of people, not an oligarchy but a heterogeneous collection of minorities. I suspect that they lived mainly in the areas of declining economic importance, and that the non-English communities in the West (Scotch and Germans) were more rather than less loyalist. I believe that they have been neglected, though Bernard Bailyn in his chapter "Contagion of Liberty" treats their ideas generously and sympathetically. I believe, however, that it was not ideas as such that led to the break with Britain, though later they were used to "intellectualize" it.

The loyalist critique is implicit in the loyalist situation of 1776 and in the fact of exile. The central point remains that in 1776 there were no "loyalists" and, outside Washington's army, not a lot of patriots either. What existed was a rebel army which it was Howe's task to destroy with as little civil fuss and fury as possible. Howe was right to assume that to destroy the army was to end the rebellion; those not in the army, he assumed, were law-abiding colonists, then loyal if not loyalist. By 1778 there was a nation in rebellion; a nation which, in part because of French intervention, but only in part for that reason, could now see a chance of total victory, with a continent, if necessary, in which to sit out time. Those who by 1778 were loyalist were thus of a different order—and suffered a different fate—from that majority of the colonists who two years before had been neutral, passive, and therefore "loyal." The study of loyalism in these crucial seven years has thus to be a study not only in semantics but also in tactics and strategy, and it needs to be tackled in depth and against a British as well as an American background. It is probably the most important aspect of the Revolution still to be tackled. And until it is tackled definitively—and its lessons understood—we shall fail to grasp that since 1776 all wars have been at once both civil and ideological struggles. In the tensions and tragedies of the loyalists, as in the tensions and tragedies of Dixie, America had its own moments of truth and its own first concern over "guilt." As the late G. N. D. Evans has shown, a study of loyalists can be used to reveal problems of loyalty, of where duty lies. This is a re-curring challenge for Americans, from Bunker Hill to Saigon. The loyalists were honest and decent men, as were the patriots, with a code quite as true. They have been called men without a country. Theirs was the greater tragedy that they were too often men with two countries, with a genuine but double allegiance, uncertain which to call home. When American loyalist ex-Governor Hutchinson died, in lonely, cold, and alien London, his heart ached for Boston. The loyalists, we should remind ourselves, were Americans too. They just guessed wrong. And in history, as in politics, as in life, you have to be on the winning side.

Note

[1] John Harvey Wheeler, *The Politics of Revolution* (Berkeley, Glendessary Press, 1971), p. 9.

Library of Congress Publications
for the
Bicentennial of the American Revolution

The American Revolution: A Selected Reading List. 1968. 38 p. 50 cents. For sale by the Superintendent of Documents, U.S. Government Printing Office, Washington, D.C. 20402.

The Boston Massacre, 1770, engraved by Paul Revere. Facsim. $1.50. For sale by the Information Office, Library of Congress, Washington, D.C. 20540.

Creating Independence, 1763–1789: Background Reading for Young People. A Selected Annotated Bibliography. 1972. 62 p. 75 cents. For sale by the Superintendent of Documents, U.S. Government Printing Office, Washington, D.C. 20402.

English Defenders of American Freedoms 1774–1778: Six Pamphlets Attacking British Policy. 1972. 231 p. $2.75. For sale by the Superintendent of Documents, U.S. Government Printing Office, Washington, D.C. 20402.

Periodical Literature on the American Revolution: Historical Research and Changing Interpretation, 1895–1970. 1971. 93 p. $1. For sale by the Superintendent of Documents, U.S. Government Printing Office, Washington, D.C. 20402.